Bush Yarns and Other Offences

CONTENTS

COPYRIGHT	ix
FOREWORD	xi
DEDICATION.	xiv

1	A Quest For Identity.	1
2	Advice From The Old Sages.	5
3	Go West Young Man!	8
4	The Longest Main Street in the World.	10
5	An Introduction To Pumpers.	16
6	Of Funerals And Inheritance.	20
7	Ray Conlan – Camooweal's Dunny Arsonist.	25
8	Leaving the Girl Of My Dreams to Return to Camooweal.	30

CONTENTS

9 | The Downside of a Copper's Marriage, He gets Transferred. 33

10 | 'Brownsville' (Townsville) - A Springboard To Something Better. 36

11 | Our First Glimpse of Laura's 'Cowsheds.' 38

12 | A Historical Re-visitation of Laura (and Maytown's) Heyday. 42

13 | A Matter Of Identity. 47

14 | A Parent's Earnest Wish. 50

15 | Bowie Gostelow's Dental Clinic. 54

16 | Fred Shephard's Christmas. 57

17 | Christmas At Laura. 59

18 | Ways and Means to Provide Meat to the Camp. 61

19 | A Novel Way to Catch Wild Pigs.. 66

20 | The Road To Dusty Death. 68

CONTENTS

21 | Some Palmerville Stories Not Recorded By History. 74

22 | Call The Flying Midwife. 78

23 | A Favour For The Flying Doctor. 80

24 | Scabies In The Camp. 82

25 | C'm 'Ere Boss, I'll Make Y're Day. 87

26 | An Ancient Mariner – Three Times Lucky On The High Seas. 89

27 | "Proper Lady Missus." 96

28 | Birthing Pains Of The Laura Rodeo. 98

29 | Managing The Heebee Jeebies. 109

30 | ^%$#@~&%$* @ (Alias Bill Jackson.) 116

31 | Power To The People. 121

32 | Mrs Holzheimer Goes for a Drive. 123

33 | Sunny Coast/Green Grass Eumundi. 127

| v |

CONTENTS

34 | What's In A Name? 129

35 | An Unshakable Family Code. 133

36 | A Trauma Shared In One Small Community. 136

37 | Bulldust, Crocs, and Salt Pan. - Burketown. 141

38 | A Small Piece Of Japan. 144

39 | A Lockup Can Be A Thirsty Place! 147

40 | How D'Ya Like Y'r Chicken - Hot or Cold? 149

41 | There Are Other Places Besides Toilet Seats To Set Up Shop. 153

42 | A Mite More Than A Belly Ache. 155

43 | Two Burketown Brothers. 159

44 | A Touch of Yellow Fever. 163

45 | Claude The Kiwi Mechanic. 167

46 | A Murderer Visits Doomadgee. 171

CONTENTS

47 | An Attempt to Satisfy an Old Bird's Fetishes. 174

48 | The Grand Political Event That Doomadgee Put On The Map. 176

49 | The Great Burketown School Fire. 179

50 | Grand Ole Granny Dawson (RIP). 181

51 | A Heavy Decision. 187

52 | An Easier Decision. 190

53 | A Bird In The Hand... 192

54 | The Attack Of The Jungle Beasts. 197

55 | Some Cow Bails Are More Than Meet The Eye. 199

56 | A Stretch Limousine For A Police Car. 202

57 | It's All A Matter Of Perspective. 206

58 | Kids In The Cop Shop. 208

59 | The 'Atherton Police Chook Cooperative.' 214

CONTENTS

Atherton Station, Old and New. 218

60 | Nothing Compares With A Doggie Diet. 220

61 | My Secret Son. 223

62 | Life Turns A Corner After Atherton. 226

The Forgotten O/c. (Officer In Charge). 229

VALE CECIL ROY AUSTEN (RIP). 231
ABOUT THE AUTHOR. 233

Bush Yarns and Other Offences

Copyright © 2022 by Max Lewis

All rights reserved. No part of this book may be reproduced in any manner whatsoever without written permission except in the case of brief quotations embodied in critical articles and reviews.

Editors: Darryl Cooper, Heather Lewis.
ISBN: 978-0-646-86038-1:
978-0-646-86045-9.
Cover design: Max Lewis
Publisher: M and H Lewis
Printed and bound in Australia by Lightening Source

Aborigines and Torres Strait Islanders are advised that the contents of this book contain images and statements of people who have died.

It will be noted that the word 'Murri' is sometimes used when referring to Aboriginal people. This is in no way a derogatory term, and in some ways more correct than 'Aborigines', since the word Murri means 'Australian Aborigine'. The word 'Murri' is used among such indigenous people by them about their kind.

The word Murri, therefore, means 'Aboriginal People of Queensland and the northern parts of New South Wales.'

Indigenous people from the southern parts of New South Wales and all parts of Victoria are correctly referred to as 'Kooris.'

FOREWORD

The work herein is the product of a reluctant writer, dragged (figuratively speaking) kicking and screaming to my keyboard by a host of 'outside influences' to produce a book of yarns.

As a result of the posting of a story or two on a social media site, I received requests from other such groups to include my tales for their groups also, which I did until my posts were reaching seven different social media sites.

In return, I received a host of expressions of pleasure and great interest from readers, along with many requests for the yarns to be converted into book form.

Initially, I resisted, but eventually, the weight of the urges prevailed.

The experiences combine to give those Country Service 'Lawmen' an interesting and sometimes exciting lifestyle as remarked upon by many who commented on the stories and yarns revealed herein.

Bush Yarns and Other Offences

A Police Officer's Initiation to Country Service by Bush Folklore

Max Lewis

Darryl Cooper, Heather Lewis (Editors)

Publisher M and H Lewis

I Dedicate This Book:

to my family:
My wife Heather,
My daughter Sharee,
And my son Brendon
Who have willingly accompanied and supported me throughout the State of Queensland to wherever
my postings have taken me. In doing so, you have, at the expense of
your own friendships...

- *Participated proudly and faithfully as members of a policing family through good times and bad.*
- *Endured my many absences 'for the Job', so frequently when you as my family really needed me at home.*
- *Been concerned for my safety, and sometimes your own – simply because I did what I did for a living, or simply because of my involvement with or on behalf of the needs of a community.*
- *You've never complained, but instead, willingly participated when necessary and where possible, in attending to someone else's needs as valuable and productive community members in your own right. I can't thank you enough.*

1

A Quest For Identity.

If having been born in a small town like Nanango (Qld) automatically makes one a bush kid, then I proudly lay claim to the title.

In all honesty though, yes, I was born in Nanango in 1944, moved to a pineapple farm at Woombye before I can remember, lived there for some five years then shifted to Nambour to stay there for about twelve months.

It was then that our family shifted to Nudgee, a suburb of Brisbane, where I lived until 22 years of age.

My schooling wasn't anything to write home about, since I disliked it with a passion. I received mediocre scores in all my grades, and my parents could see no purpose in making me stay after my Scholarship (Grade 8) exam.

They allowed me to leave school to find work at the tender age of 14 in the year 1957.

I was obviously too young to take responsibility and properly hold down a job, and it wasn't until the mid-1960s that I finally matured sufficiently to be an asset to my working environment.

In fact, I was immensely proud to give notice at my job when leaving to join the Queensland Police, since it was the only job of many that I'd had, where I gave notice and hadn't been asked to leave.

It was after I turned 21 years of age in April 1966 that I left home to commence my training as a Police Officer with the Queensland Police Force, - the beginning of the adventure of my life.

Therefore, I now must face the truth and reluctantly agree with those observers who would have wished to label me as a 'townie' or a 'city bloke'.

Since by far most of the stories and yarns I mean to relate herein have seen their geneses in the bush and small police stations attached thereto, I shall spend little time describing my policing service in the cities.

Nevertheless, I consider it necessary to relate the various Stations where I served, in order that one might gather a perspective of the order of and length of time spent in the various towns wherein we lived and became members of those communities.

The squad in which I trained at the Police Depot, Petrie Terrace Brisbane, was sworn in, on 30th June 1966. I was immediately posted to Clayfield Station, and it is therefore at Clayfield where I commenced my Policing career. Only three months later I was transferred to Roma Street Station, Brisbane, to again meet up with many of my colleagues from my training squad.

Author's Police Swearing In Parade, 30 June 1966. Parade Sergeant, Tom Molloy; Taking the Salute, Premier Joh Bjelke Petersen.
Queensland Police Photographic Unit.

Most of us were posted to what some referred to as 'the fattening paddock' before being transferred to a more permanent position. This, I guess was to have one last look at a new recruit's suitability for the job prior to transferring to a more permanent position somewhere in the rest of the State to continue through their final confirmation as a fully-fledged police officer after 12 months service.

2

Advice From The Old Sages.

I spent the bulk of my duty at Roma Street Station, driving the 'Drunks Van' or if you prefer, the Paddy Wagon. This had a three-man crew comprising myself, a Senior Constable, and a Sergeant in Charge – Sergeant Neil.

Now Neil was at heart, a country police officer and he was to give me some excellent advice that would influence my career for the full 33 years of service within the police ranks. Speaking from a perspective of having served a good many years in and around Longreach in the central west of Queensland, Neil said, "If you want a fulfilling career in the Police service then get yourself a CPS Station and do some service in the bush."

CPS stands for Clerk of Petty Sessions, (now called Clerk of the Court) and a principal difference between working at a larger centre and a CPS station is that in the smaller places, the Police are almost always the only State Government office in town.

That being so, the police are obliged to attend, not only to their policing duties but also to represent other State bodies. Departments such as State Transport Dept. (Issuing of Drivers Licenses); Main Roads Dept. (Motor Vehicle Registration).

Roma Street Police Station 1967. Demolished the early 1970s to make way for an overpass. (Unknown Photographer).

Also, Court of Petty Sessions, - keeping and processing of Court Records; and on occasions acting as Prosecutor should the Magistrate convene a court in your town.

Following the advice of my Sergeant, I approached the District Officer at the Roma Street Station after about six months of service there and asked to be transferred to a CPS Station anywhere in the State.

Now the advice that Sergeant Neil handed to me on that occasion, was only one of several gems from his store of wisdom, and it somehow picked up my thinking, over another not-so-bright nugget previously handed to me by another Sergeant.

This person was a law lecturer at the Police Depot. The Sergeant seemed to be stuck in an antiquated belief system that suggested, that before you could be something, you had to be something else. It seems to have been a relic of the British Colonial times, and the Sergeant still believed it to be valid.

How he knew I still don't understand, but for a moment it struck me with disappointment, however, I took the message on board but set about my career with an aim to succeed despite what he had told me.

The bright piece of information was, "Max, you understand that you are not going to go far in the Police Force because to do so you need to be either a Catholic or a Freemason, and I see that you are neither."

I never saw nor heard of the Sergeant again in the Job, and he may have progressed past the rank of Sergeant, but I have never seen his name among those who did really succeed, and let's say finally that my career achievement took me significantly higher than that of Sergeant, despite my
'so-called' personal deficiencies.

A drunks van similar to that used by the Queensland Police Department in the late 1960s. (Photographer unknown).

3

Go West Young Man!

Within a very short period, I found myself transferred to Mount Isa, and I also learned that one of my Police Depot mates, Terry Price (RIP) was transferred to Cloncurry at the same time.

Mount Isa Police Station 1967. Demolished 1969 to make way for new structure opened 1970
Queensland Police Force Photographic Section.

Terry and I decided to travel together in our own respective private vehicles for mutual safety and assurance.

On the day we left, Terry drove in the lead out of Brisbane with me following close behind and heading west towards Roma.

Everything was smooth sailing until we reached Dalby, and while driving steadily through the town, somehow or other Terry had an accident with another vehicle and badly damaged his utility.

We were very fortunate in that I was driving a large car, a 1958 model Ford Customline, which had sufficient room for both of us and our gear, so after Terry had attended to the necessary details over the traffic incident and stowed the car at the Dalby Police Station, we continued on our way.

Now, having two drivers in one vehicle, we were able to drive nonstop throughout the night and we arrived at Cloncurry the next day. I dropped Terry off and continued to Mount Isa. After due time to acclimatise, and for my sinus passages to grow used to the sulfuric fumes emanating from Mount Isa Mines, I soon began to enjoy working there.

This was so because I found myself working with a good bunch of fellow Police and living in the Police Barracks alongside them.

4

The Longest Main Street in the World.

Before that year was out, I was advised by the Officer in Charge of the Police Station, Senior Sergeant Ken that I was required to relieve at Camooweal Station for three months.

It came as quite a surprise, since the only thing I knew about Camooweal apart from being the last town before the Northern Territory Border, was that it was jokingly described as having the longest main street in the world. This refers to the fact that although 189.9 kilometres from Mount Isa, it was still a part of the Mount Isa Shire Council.

Here, out of the blue arrived my sought-after opportunity to work at my first CPS Station, having just one other Police Officer in the town in the person of Sergeant Don (RIP).

Although not long out of my traineeship period he gave me full freedom to drive unaccompanied to surrounding cattle station properties and conduct all necessary police inquiries unsupervised. I believe we operated well together, and I began to envy Constable John (RIP), his permanent work partner, at that time, absent on leave.

Camooweal Police Station 1967. Said to have been formerly a woolshed. Demolished in the early 1970s.
Photo: Max Lewis

oOo

It was in the very early hours of the morning, (perhaps three or four o'clock) when Don received word of a serious road accident that had occurred some 80 km or so out of Camooweal, on the road to Mount Isa. Still waking ourselves up, we climbed into our Ford Falcon Utility Police car and drove to the scene, where it was quite apparent that an older model Holden had struck a road train head-on, completely wrecking the Holden.

The car had obviously been packed to the gunnels with clothing and other household gear because the contents were strewn all about the crash scene.

Once we had climbed from our vehicle, we learned that the male driver was deceased, and his female passenger was badly injured, conscious but barely coherent. It soon became apparent that they were a young married couple, packed and travelling to Darwin. The driver had likely gone to sleep at the wheel and swerved into the path of the road train.

The small group of people, which included an Ambulance Bearer was attempting to comfort the injured young woman who appeared to be repeatedly calling out something that nobody at that time could understand. As the young woman became more conscious, her words gradually became more coherent, and we eventually understood that she was calling out for her baby.

Nobody was aware there was a baby present and a thorough search was made inside the car as well as outside among the strewn personal items around the wreckage. No baby was found, and we began to feel that the woman may have been hallucinating

Someone, a member of the searching group then managed to open the car boot, and, surprisingly, lying therein was a young baby. Sadly, the child was deceased.

Subsequent inquiries revealed that earlier in the evening the mother had been nursing the baby until it went to sleep, and because the motor vehicle was so packed, the only place she could lay the young child was on the ledge behind the rear seat, and there it was at the time of the collision.

It was theorized that at the time of the collision, the baby's weight had sprung the 'backrest' of the rear seat forward allowing the baby to drop down into the boot. A later inspection of the rear seat showed that indeed, the 'squab' of the seat was detached allowing it to spring forward.

Sergt. Don decided that I should take both bodies in the utility to the Mount Isa Hospital morgue while he remained at the crash site.

I placed the deceased baby on the passenger seat beside me, and with the assistance of others present, we lifted the deceased male into the rear bed of the utility.

The deceased was quite a tall man, and even though we slid his upper body as far forward as possible, his feet just protruded from the rear of the utility thus preventing our closing the tailgate.

I found that by bending his knees a little I could get the tailgate closed, after which I could then push his knees down and they would 'lock' and stay in the straight position.

I discovered that I needed the knees in the 'down position' because when bent they could be seen protruding above the utility side, indicating to those who may have been paying attention that I had a human body lying in the tray of the Police vehicle.

I left the scene just as dawn was breaking, and after a few kilometres, I looked into the rear-view mirror and noticed that my passenger's knees had again popped up.

I reasoned that I could make it to the outskirts of Mount Isa without too much concern for how we looked and that by then the road would be smoother and less likely to 'bump' up the knees as had the rougher highway.

That is what I did, and as I reached the outskirts, I stopped the vehicle, pushed the knees down, and proceeded carefully into the higher volume of traffic.

To those who know Mount Isa, you would be aware that where the highway meets the northern outlet of the Marian Street bridge the intersection can be quite busy, and I happened to be arriving there at 'morning peak hour'.

Watching the traffic action ahead, I could see that I was going to have to pull up for other traffic, and I was in the left lane of a two-lane piece of road. There was a large truck stationary in the right-hand lane and other traffic behind me.

Lo and behold, to my horror I rolled over an undulation in the roadway and glancing in the mirror I watched two knees spring into the air. I am praying, "Please Mr Truckie, don't look over my way".

Well, that was one prayer that I'm pleased to say was answered, because the truck driver remained blissfully unaware, and I was pleased to make my way to the hospital, even though for that distance, two knees hung above the side of the utility for everyone to see.

5

An Introduction To Pumpers.

Another task soon after my arrival was to drive out to Carpentaria Downs Station to bring back to town a "pumper" whose name now eludes me. The man was quite ill. On arrival, I beheld a very dirty, emaciated old man who was so ill he couldn't walk to the police car - a 1965 Ford Falcon Ute.

The old guy was loaded into the passenger seat of the Falcon, and he was duly transported to the Camooweal hospital. I have to say that the smell was horrendous.

At the hospital, the Nursing Sisters felt it necessary to give him a bath, and when undressing him peeled seven singlets from his skinny old frame. Had he been in the city, he would have been passed off as 'just another vagrant', but here he was, in employment at a large cattle property.

I wondered what work he was able to do to earn his wages, and what skills were required to earn the 'professional title' of "Pumper"?

Not all that long after, I was at the Camooweal pub when I saw a man at the bar who had the biggest stomach I had ever seen.

On my inquiry as to his identity, the publican, Biddie Conlan (RIP). said, "Oh that's Popeye, he's a pumper from Rocklands, and he's come to town for his holidays. We put him up in the drunks room. Just watch out, Max, this is going to be an interesting week."

My first question of Biddie was, "First of all, what is a pumper, and why is this week going to be interesting?"

She said, "Pumpers are almost always burnt-out alcoholics who a cattle station will employ to live in a remote corner of the property. Their only role is to kick over the diesel engine on a bore pump when a dam needs replenishing. The only other human contact is the driver of the station truck that brings him weekly supplies and fuel for the engine. Sometimes they'll sneak him a bottle of rum to keep him happy."

"Now Popeye has been out at his pump for the last 12 months, and he is now in town for two weeks of annual holidays. He hands his holiday pay cheque to me to look after, keep a tally, and then tell him when it's spent. He then returns to his bore pump for another year. The first week he will be constantly drunk, in the D.Ts, and generally making a nuisance of himself. The next week he will be sober, drinking heavily, but impossible to fill up".

True to form, that evening, just as the weekly dance was getting properly underway, Popeye decided to take his shower. He already had a bellyful of 'juice'.

Now he was so obese that he needed to have a chair placed in the shower to sit on while he put his pants on. It wasn't until he'd finished his shower that he realized that his chair was missing.

His 'bath robe' was an old military great coat that sported a split in the rear that went right up to his shoulder blades, thus allowing his huge backside to protrude through the split like a hippo's posterior.

The logistical problem he had was that in order to get from the shower to his room, it was necessary to work his way through the revellers on the dance floor.

These were not all locals, but most were tourists and travellers who were travelling to Darwin on the Red Line Coach.

The first hint of anything unusual was Popeye's plaintive cries of 'Yaaa,' 'Yaaa', 'Yaaa' as he crossed the dance floor with Biddie poking at his bare behind with the cattle-jigger she always kept under the bar counter for just such an occasion.

Aside: Popeye was so large and heavy that he couldn't be lifted by normal means should he 'choke' down on the floor. Locals commonly witnessed the Police employing the services of the Council's front-end loader to transport him to the Watchhouse. They would place the loader bucket beside him and roll him into it. Thus, accommodated he would enjoy a unique aerial ride to the lockup.

The outdoor Movie Theatre, Camooweal 1967
Photo: Max Lewis

6

Of Funerals And Inheritance.

Isn't it great how, when the chips are down, people seem to come out of the woodwork to help?

There was an old tumbledown, deserted shack at Camooweal when I was there in 1967.

This hovel became the shelter for all and sundry, these usually being itinerants passing through, and the odd down-and-out alcoholic.

At this material time, the shack was in the grasp of an old skinny alcoholic whose name has now vanished in the mists of time. Still, he was recognized by his other down and out colleagues as the 'owner' of the joint because he had been there the longest, and others were simply 'guests'.

One morning this would be 'landlord' woke up dead and my workmate John and I were awakened by one of the 'guests' of this 'landlord' who told us that the old bloke had died in his sleep.

Our inspection of both the body and the scene revealed no grounds for suspicion, and we transported the body up to the hospital where we locked it in a shed, there being no official morgue, and of course no body fridge.

The hospital sister had already contacted the Flying Doctor in Mount Isa and learned the Doctor was happy to issue a Certificate of Cause of Death based on the deceased's recent medical history, which allowed us to make immediate arrangements for his burial.

There being no known next of kin we wondered who would be paying the funeral expenses.

Wonder of wonders, the old guy who had reported the death told us that he was willing to bear all expenses, but that for now he would need to raise a temporary loan.

The only one local that we knew could grant a loan was a local shopkeeper, Joe Freckelton, (RIP), a guy so frugal that our down-and-out friend would stand no chance whatever of securing a loan.

Having serious doubts as to the future success of our mission, we went to Joe's shop and began serious negotiations on our friend's behalf.

Miraculously Joe knew our client well and readily undertook to cover a loan for all expenses. It was now up to us to purchase the cemetery plot and to pick a casket also on hand at the Council, to place the deceased therein.

The only things left to do now were to find someone in the town to conduct the funeral service, there being no local clergy, and then have the burial service. John was at a loss as to who was appropriate to conduct the service, so I took the problem to another shop owner, an ex-police officer named Jack Moloney. Jack's quick answer was "That's your job".

I was immediately taken aback, being a Police Officer with barely twelve months of service, and someone, who had only been in the town (temporarily) for a couple of those months, faced with a problem like this.

After a quick nervous intake of breath, I said, "Now Jack, can I ask, if I wasn't here, who would be doing the burial?"

He said, "Well in that case I usually do them".

I found it difficult to hide my relief.

We set the funeral for 2 pm that afternoon and went to the hospital and its 'morgue', where we placed the deceased into the casket.

It was here that we found another practical use for a Police Utility truck: It became a makeshift hearse.

We drove around the block of Camooweal thus giving the drinkers at the pub time to finish their drinks and load up into their cars in time for a funeral procession behind the 'police hearse' and drive to the cemetery to say their last farewells to their deceased friend.

And that, my friends, is how by chance, the dear departed, received a Catholic funeral, rather than the honour of a Protestant burial, had I been cajoled into conducting it.

During my police service, I did get to conduct several funeral services, but some of those stories are for another time.

I found out soon after the above funeral that our benevolent friend who stood the cost of the funeral did so for the purpose of becoming the new 'owner' of the abandoned shack.

(Well at least they didn't try to occupy the Picture Theatre!)

The 'lounge bar' of the Camooweal Movie Theatre, 1967
Photo: Max Lewis

1967 saw a quite serious rat plague in the northwest. Sitting in the Camooweal Picture theatre watching the weekly movie, I was dressed in my shorts and thongs and felt a nibbling at the edge of my big toe. Looking down I saw a large rat having a tentative nibble before taking a larger chomp. I learned to watch my feet from then on.

7

Ray Conlan – Camooweal's Dunny Arsonist.

The Post Office Hotel, (Better known as 'The Camooweal Pub') 1967. Destroyed by fire in the Early 1970s, replaced soon after by a modern timber structure. Photo: Max Lewis

A 'character' about whom I have been promising myself to write is that of Ray Conlan (RIP), husband of Biddie Conlan

(RIP), who was the Licensee of the Camooweal Hotel during the sixties and seventies.

Ray stood in as a general roustabout, maintenance man, barman, bouncer, and general verbal entertainer; whichever was called for at any given time.

One of the sources of my enjoyment during that time was to sit on the edge of the boardwalk of the pub and listen to Ray's yarns and 'cracks' about various local people.

One of the victims of his cracks was Camooweal's Joe Freckleton (RIP), a local storekeeper who was reputed to be extremely frugal with his money. One of Ray's cracks at Joe went as follows...

Joe one day was feeling a little unwell, to the degree that he went to see the Flying Doctor. The Doctor ran several tests and finally told Joe that he had sugar in his urine. Without delay, Joe raced home and peed in the custard.

Often was the time that a gullible tourist would turn up at the Police Station and ask to play pool on our table, having been told by Ray that we were a Snooker Parlour.

One turned up with an anxious look on his face, looking for the local prostitute, and so, on it went.

A problem of Ray's was that he used to break out occasionally on the booze, getting so drunk for so long that he went into the horrors.

He would either become violent, wanting to fight any or everybody, (and that was dangerous since he apparently had a former history of ring boxing); or he'd take it out on the pub.

On one occasion he took to the hotel with an axe, and on another occasion saw him trying to burn it down. Fortunately, he never succeeded in either endeavour., although, in the early 1970s the old pub did in fact catch alight and burn to the ground. I am unable to say if there were suspicious circumstances, since, by then I had moved to Townsville.

I have always been a 'non-drinker' and here I had what was called a 'Max Special', 2/3 glass of orange juice, 1/3 of ginger ale.

On 'Red Line Coach nights', I would take my trumpet to help form a band at the pub, and on these evenings, I was supplied with as many 'Max Specials' as I desired.

One night, I believe Ray slipped some vodka into the drinks, and that night I do not remember going home. Fortunately, there were no calls for police service.

Camooweal, like so many western towns, from time to time – not every year, gets seriously plagued by gidgee bugs. Grey, shield-shaped bugs that smell worse than a camel's underarm in summer, should you crush one such insect.

They would arrive out of nowhere and, being attracted to light would swarm around those lights that by necessity were left switched on overnight.

The Police Station 'Single Men's Quarters' comprised a single bedroom round the rear but part of the main building, which at that time was built from bush sawn timber covered with corrugated iron.

John, being the permanent member when I later went to Camooweal to relieve when the Sergeant took his leave, occupied the bedroom, which meant that I slept on a bed set up on the open verandah.

During the gidgee bug 'visitation', trying to sleep was particularly daunting, since the beetles would land on the bed covers with a 'plonk' and try their darndest to weasel their way in.

Of course, to roll over on one was not a good idea, but if they found you first, they would bite, which, though not venomous was still sharp enough to hurt.

Their swarm would usually last one night (sometimes more) and the next morning they would have to be cleaned from wherever they settled by any means available.

The Camooweal public toilets were painted white and were lit externally all night by two 40-watt fluorescent lights. The morning after a 'visitation', the council workers scraped enough bugs to fill two 44-gallon rubbish bins with them.

The pub had its own public toilets, in the form of outside 'dunnies' built of galvanised iron. The only timber bits were the building frame and the toilet seats. The gidgee bugs were no match for Ray's method of dealing with them; throw flammable liquid on the outside iron, and set a match to it. The bugs didn't stand a chance.

Although, for anyone standing downwind of the fire the shrivelling bug-odour wafting from the inferno was really something to transport you to another realm. Of course, it necessitated repainting the dunnies before they rusted, but, every two or so years wasn't really such a bad thing.

I am sure that in the general scheme of things, God places people like Ray Conlan in and around small western areas to lighten the load of hardship and sometimes boredom, for the benefit of the hardy souls who inhabit these wonderful small bush towns

8

Leaving the Girl Of My Dreams to Return to Camooweal.

It was during this period back at home base, that I met Heather, the girl who would later become my wife.

I have to say that our feelings for each other were very strong, so much so that when Senior Sergeant Ken signaled that he wanted me to do another stint of one month at Camooweal, I was not particularly keen to go.

John, who was then acting Officer-in-Charge in the absence of Sergeant Don, who with his wife and family were now on their leave, very kindly gave me rest days every second weekend. So I religiously made the 180 km trip to Mount Isa for those two rest days to see Heather.

It was during my return to Camooweal late one Sunday night that something quite unusual occurred. The road was almost devoid of traffic and as I reached a point just on the Camooweal side of halfway, I entered a long stretch of straight road and something significant in the headlights caught my eye.

Closer in I saw that it was a motorcycle lying in the middle of the bitumen road. I stopped and saw that there was no rider in the immediate vicinity. Turning my car in a wide circle, I noticed the carcass of a 3/4 grown bull lying off to the side of the road, but about 20 meters from the motorcycle, in the direction of Mount Isa.

Looking past the dead beast but in that same direction, I came across the cycle rider lying about 10 meters further on. Closer inspection of the male person revealed that he was still alive, but barely conscious.

His limbs appeared uninjured, and the only obvious injury was that he appeared to have lost all the skin from one side of his face, no doubt caused by his 'skating' on his face across the coarse bitumen.

I could see that he was slowly becoming more conscious as time went by, and once the guy had 'come' to a little more I found that he was able to stand up with my assistance and eventually walked to the car and installed himself in the passenger seat.

I managed to stand the motorcycle up and push it over to the side of the road. I left it semi-concealed behind a small grove of trees to await daylight when it could be retrieved.

We traveled to Camooweal where I left the young man with the Nursing Sister who then arranged for his transportation by ambulance to Mount Isa.

I learned later that although the peeled-back skin and flesh injury went almost to the facial bones, most of the flesh and skin were still present and lying folded down under the jawbone.

The Mount Isa hospital doctors were able to stretch and stitch it back into place without too much difficulty.

The young man spent only a brief period in hospital and was able to then leave, proudly sporting a brand new set of jawline scars.

9

The Downside of a Copper's Marriage, He gets Transferred.

I would spend the next three years at Mount Isa performing General Duties Policing, and for a significant period running the Traffic Office. This meant testing for and issuing driver's licenses, and inspecting motor vehicles for which an application was being made for Registration. In addition to that, I was inspecting motor vehicles over which a defect notice had been issued, where the fault had now been rectified.

My relationship with Heather blossomed during this period, and eventually, we decided to be married. The wedding took place and for the young Police Officers who found themselves invited, there arose a dilemma.

Our wedding was to be 'dry', meaning no alcohol, and boys being boys, the Police could see themselves dying of thirst having to last that long at a celebration trying to quench their thirst with cups of tea/coffee, punch, or soft drink.

A group of fellow police officers attached to Mount Isa Station during the period prior to 1970 during which I was stationed there. (from left) John Enright, Dick Nicola, Shaun Molloy, Terry Price (RIP), Barrie Johnson (RIP) John Fox (RIP) Ray Findlay, Ross Dwyer. (Photographer Unknown)

The problem was eventually easily solved by their treating the whole affair like a football match, wherein there was no drinking until 'half time' (the break between the wedding ceremony and the reception).

They were then able to make the time to slip down to the pub to treat their cracking skin and be back well before the Bride and Groom had returned from their photo session.

The Police Force at the time always worked on a principle of cause and consequence, and because of our marriage, we were transferred to Townsville.

Although I was allowed to choose three Police Stations to which I would prefer to be transferred, I was sent to Townsville - not one of the three.

10

'Brownsville' (Townsville) - A Springboard To Something Better.

Still a Constable at this stage I commenced General Duties in Townsville, usually driving a patrol vehicle in the City centre and some closer-in suburbs, with a Sergeant sitting in the passenger seat beside me.

After only a few months in General Duties, I was asked to go upstairs to become a Police Clerk in the District Inspector's office.

Although not keen to be out of the action, I realized that I was receiving excellent experience in what was at that time a rather complex and cumbersome system of document handling. I told myself that this would stand me in good stead once I became the Officer in Charge of my own Station.

It was 1974, and we now were the parents of two young children.

I had been applying for transfers to small stations, and I was sure that my Sergeant in charge of the Office in which I worked was somehow placing the kybosh on my applications, not wanting me to leave. I figured 'Well if I were to apply for a position that very few other Police in Queensland would want, I should stand a fair chance of snagging it.

So I applied for Laura.

When the transfer came through, I rang Heather and said to her; "We've got Laura."

She said: "Who's Laura?" (even though we had discussed and agreed to the lodging of the application, and some of what I knew we would face).

When I explained it to her, she went quiet, and I still don't know what went through her mind at that moment, (remembering that she was born and grew up in Mount Isa and had a pretty good idea of what it was like to be living in that kind of 'multi-cultured environment).

11

Our First Glimpse of Laura's 'Cowsheds.'

Upon our arrival at Laura, Heather found it hard to believe that it was an actual town since from the main road it resembled a collection of buildings not unlike you would find at a large grazing property.

In we went, and it takes no stretch of the imagination to realize that we didn't need to ask for directions to the Police Station and residence, since it comprised of a house set apart from the four other buildings in the town—the Shop, Pub, Dance Hall and School. At that time there were no Aborigine homes although they arrived sometime after we became settled in the town.

Peninsular Development Road, Laura Turnoff, 1997
Photo: Heather Lewis

The Murries at that time lived in shacks on the bank of the Laura River, quite separate from the town.

My predecessor, Senr. Constable Herb (RIP) was not at the house, but everything was wide open so we took the liberty of inspecting the residence to move his furniture out ready for it to be taken away in the truck that had brought our gear.

Imagine our surprise when all we found in the house was one swag, and a huge pile of clothes on top of a blanket sitting on the floor of the second bedroom.

Sharee, our eldest child, 2 years of age went for her tour of inspection and found her way into the bathroom. There soon came a yell from her, since her little fingers had found Herb's 'stash' of used Blue Gillette razor blades and come away from the room streaming blood from a razor cut to her hand. We shifted our gear inside, and some time later, Herb turned up, confirming that he had no furniture to speak of, picking up the blanket full of clothes, threw it in the back of his car with his dog, and drove away to his new posting at Cairns.

I had, before leaving Townsville, learned that there was an Aboriginal Tracker attached to Laura Station, and we were keen to make our acquaintance with George Musgrave (RIP). George, and his wife, Kathy (RIP). would become good friends with Heather and me and of course, they grew popular with both our young children as they grew older.

Four Wheel Drive, Toyota Land Cruiser Police vehicle, Laura.
Photographer Unknown

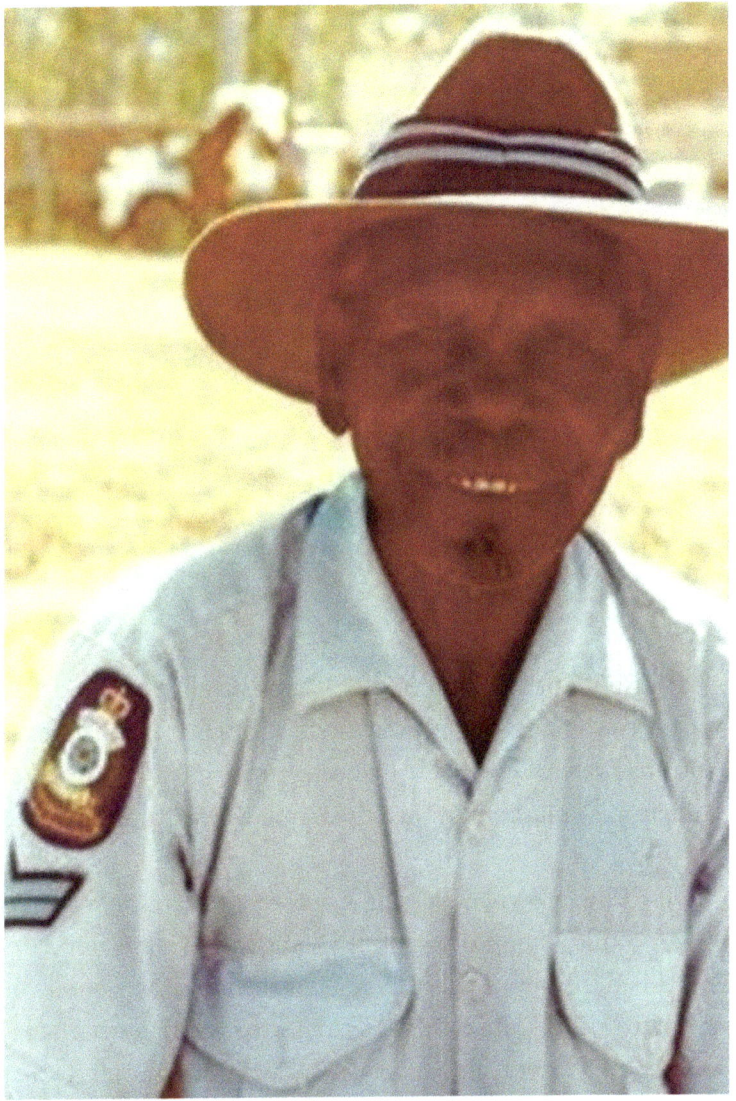

Queensland Police Tracker (retired) George Musgrave (RIP)
Photo: Max Lewis.

12

A Historical Re-visitation of Laura (and Maytown's) Heyday.

It wasn't until I'd joined the Queensland Police and later transferred to Laura Station that my Dad advised me that he had a cousin, Evelyn Lewis (RIP) who had married a Police Officer and that this Police Officer had died somewhere around Laura.

'Maybe he drowned crossing a river, or perhaps he was taken by a crocodile.' The story sounded too good to leave alone, and when I had the opportunity to contact the Police Museum, who conducted the research, they later reported the following which at a later time I wrote into a Lewis Family History book.

Here is that story... On 1 April 1923, Elijah, who preferred to be called Frank was inducted into the Queensland Police Force and initially served at Roma Street (Brisbane) and Maryborough police stations.

He was posted to Nanango on 13 May 1924 and found himself married to Evelyn Lewis, 11 months later.

Soon after their marriage, Frank was posted to Rockhampton and the young couple relocated there.

They had no sooner arrived in Rockhampton than Frank was again posted, this time to Maytown, - a small mining town, in the Palmer River gold area west of Cooktown.

Evelyn, who was at an advanced stage of pregnancy with their first child remained in Cairns while Frank made his way by boat from Cairns to Cooktown, and then by train to Laura. Ahead he was looking at a probable three-day trek by horse over a rough mountainous road to Maytown.

By the time Frank arrived at Laura he was quite ill, to the extent that the Laura Police Officer suggested he take sick leave and return to Cooktown to see a doctor.

Young Frank, no doubt eager to reach his posting did not accept the advice and after a short rest at Laura, set out for Maytown.

By the time he reached his destination he was very ill, so much so, it is reported, he was unable to 'get about'.

He decided to try to return to Laura and then to Cooktown to take the advice of his workmate, however, he was too ill to ride and was therefore carried by Aborigines on a stretcher. (In those times the Police Force employed several 'black trackers' who assisted the Police Officers in various ways.)

Frank was likely carried by Aboriginal Trackers. They carried Frank over the miles from Maytown towards Laura, and it was while they were crossing the almost dry Laura Riverbed about two miles short of Laura that Frank died.

Rusting ancient gold stamp machinery at Maytown 1976.
Photo: Max Lewis

His body was kept at the Laura Police station while a casket was built at Cooktown and transported by rail to Laura. An outer box was also ordered in which to place the casket (and body) to disguise the fact that a deceased person was being transported.

When the train carrying the body eventually arrived at Cooktown station, the local hearse was present to transport the body. Although the original intention was to disguise the fact of the presence of a dead body, the need to save Government money prevailed, so they decided to dispense with all caution and use the hearse anyway.

Unfortunately, the outer box covering the coffin refused to fit inside the hearse, causing a situation whereby the Cooktown Police were required to dutifully report the fact that it was necessary to expend more Government finances hiring a dray to transport the 'consignment' from the train station to the wharf.

All then went without incident and Frank Taylor's remains were taken by the ship 'Malanda' and later interred in the Cairns cemetery.

Evelyn was still in Cairns and gave birth to a baby girl on 22 November 1925. She named the baby 'Norma Jean Taylor'. They would subsist on a Police Departmental Pension allowance of sixty pounds per year for Evelyn plus twenty- six pounds per year for the baby.

Sadly, the baby died two years later, on 24 November 1927.

Evelyn would travel south working as a waitress in hotels and restaurants in Mitchell (Qld), New farm (Brisbane), Marburg, and as far south as Sydney.

In 1936, while Evelyn lived at Newfarm, her mother Sarah came to live for a short time in a flat in nearby Brunswick Street, Newfarm.

Sarah would remain there until relocating to live with William (Evelyn's brother) in George Street, Brisbane. Evelyn died in Brisbane on 30 September 1980.

MAX LEWIS

13

A Matter Of Identity.

Although very common in the seventies, it sometimes occurs to this day that an indigenous person, when required to sign a document will request to use a right thumbprint, in which instance the person requesting the 'signature' will make available a stamp pad, and the 'signee' will thereby ink their thumbprint and leave their mark beside an inscription written by the receiver 'Mark of' - and the name of the person 'signing' the document.

A tragic truism in a recent generation of Aborigine's life is often the transition into the high-tech world that wishes to know everything about individuals when said indigenes simply do not possess those details purely because they were never recorded in the first place.

An oldish Aboriginal ringer from the western side of Cape York Peninsular came to my office at Laura on one occasion with something heavy weighing him down.

I spoke to him about general items of mutual interest for a time, until the nub of his question was ready to appear, and he said, "Sergeant, can you tell me, how old am I?"

Now Police Stations carry many and various records, but not that kind of information, at least not in those days. I remained serious, stood up, and walked over to one of our old charge books which is an ancient-looking, large, leather-bound record book.

I opened it as though I was searching, and then said to him, Henry you are 53, and born on ../../.. I wrote it down for him, and he left my office as happy as Larry, proudly carrying his precious piece of paper and feeling fulfilled in his mission.

It is interesting how to some, these details are important, while to others it matters very little.

George Musgrave, for the years he was employed by the Police Department as a Police Tracker never expressed any interest in such matters.

Not long after we arrived in Laura, Heather queried, "George, how old would you be?" To which George replied "Uh, I be about forty or fifty Missus"

We returned to Laura for the Rodeo in 1997, (23 years after our first arrival) and by this time, George had retired.

While sitting under a shady tree and chatting with George, Heather asked: "George, how old would you be now?"

George replied, "Uh, I be about forty or fifty Missus."

A great, lasting memory of George!

14

A Parent's Earnest Wish.

Heather and I arrived in Laura in 1974, just a young couple with a 2-year-old girl (Sharee) and a babe in arms (Brendon). Of course, as young parents, we had high ideals for what our children should see and experience.

Knowing what can and does happen at any Police Station, what with drunks, bad language, naked women fighting in the front yard, and the odd lowlife to deal with, we held grave concerns as to how this environment may influence the healthy development and outlook of our children.

The substance of our concerns arrived soon after... An aeroplane 'load' of Aurukun citizens arrived with the intention of 'doing a grog run.' In other words, purchasing liquor and taking it back illegally to Aurukun. Percy Trezise (RIP), who was both publican and pilot was very willing to sell them the grog but told them quite forcibly that there would be no drinking in the aeroplane on the homeward journey. The first suggestion of trouble I had was when the pub staff rang me to say that the 'grog-runner' passengers had started drinking on board and that Percy was returning to Laura.

I met the plane at the airfield and made the passengers empty the liquor onto the ground, after which I loaded them up, arresting each individual for being drunk. Unloading them at the watch house, one of them wished to have a frank exchange of ideas over the situation, and when that failed he raised his fists. To protect myself I was obliged to knock him down. He came up fighting and I again assisted him in quickly locating the ground. I finally got them all into the watchhouse and shut the door.

Glancing down at the house, I could clearly see a pair of two-year-old blue eyes watching everything that had occurred. I went home and told Heather what had transpired, and we felt that our worst fears had now been realised. It took another twelve hours for our fears to be allayed, and the answer to our perceived problem to materialise.

The next morning I had the prisoners lined up in the Police Station which at that time was in the front room of the house. Soon I could hear the approaching footsteps of our two-year-old Sharee. Without hesitation she picked out the 'fighting hero', and looking him in the eye she said, "You was naughty yesterday, my daddy had to give you a smack." We were never concerned about the issue again, and our kids have now grown up none the worse off for having spent all of their formative years in and around Police Stations.

George Musgrave, Nancy (his sister-in-law), Sharee, and George's children. (Photo: Heather Lewis.)

15

Bowie Gostelow's Dental Clinic.

It took only a short time in town before we met Bowie Gostellow RIP. – (nicknamed after Ben Bowyang), a recent owner of the Laura Store and now a contract linesman caring for the overland, single wire telephone line.

Bowie's kit was his Landrover utility carrying a ladder, in the rear tray a chainsaw, axe, reaping hook, digging tools and toolbox.

The toolbox, showing the weight of years of hard work trying to keep its contents together while being humped and bumped over atrocious roads, and often across country on horseback.

The box contained many varied tools all knocked about by those same elements that had reduced the toolbox to its current state.

The notable item in the box was a pair of tooth extractors (the authentic dentist's item) that he had carried about ever since his droving days.

Should one of his drovers develop toothache on the track, Bowie would boil the extractors in his billycan and perform the operation there and then cold turkey. If the patient was fortunate, he could be medicated by a belly full of Bundy Rum. Bowie claimed to have used the extractors many times over the years.

A tourist 'cityite' on one occasion called into the pub and complained that he had a serious toothache and was looking for a dentist.

The flash visitor was quickly referred next door to Bowie who, at the time was the owner of the Laura Store, and Bowie, ever the obliging one, jumped at the chance to help.

He went to his faithful toolbox which was stowed in the rear of his Landrover and retrieved the trusty/rusty implement and dropped it into his billycan.

When the townie saw what was happening, he chucked a mickey, jumped out of the chair and drove all the way back to Mareeba to find relief.

Unfortunately, it is unlikely that Bowie was ever paid for that 'consultation'.

oOo

Now it was Laura Race weekend and the whole district was visiting and tonight attending the Race Ball - except one. Bowie's brother, Miles (RIP), had enjoyed a big day and decided to stay in camp with his bottle of Bundy.

The race ball was in full swing when Miles arrived with Bundy-flavoured blood in his eye. He was certain that his wife, Connie (RIP) was playing up with someone other than himself. In a jealous rage, he staggered across the dance floor and confronted Connie.

As chance would have it, she was dancing with her own brother, Kevin Callaghan (RIP), however, it required more than a deal of rowdy persuasion to convince Miles that his wife was remaining faithful to him.

Now there are times when the prudent Police Officer needs to busy him/herself elsewhere, so reluctantly I disappeared to allow familial law to have its way without interference.

As I heard it told afterwards, all the rest of the male members of the Gostelow clan escorted Miles outside and stood around in a circle while Bowie administered summary justice, laying Miles out cold.

Dutifully then, the young male members of the clan carried Miles' unconscious body over to the ute, throwing him into the back, they delivered him back to the camp.

16

Fred Shephard's Christmas.

Fred Shephard (RIP), his wife Ruth (RIP), and their family members are prominent graziers on the Cape York Peninsula. The greater Shephard family (Fred's parents and his siblings), owned properties, mainly situated on The Cape, and have contributed to the good of that area for generations.

It is well known that Fred spent his whole life on the Peninsula, living his early life at Musgrave which during his childhood would have been a remote and lonely outpost indeed, seeing few unfamiliar faces, and quite innocent of any knowledge or understanding of the goings on in the outside world.

Fred had cause to visit the Laura Police Station a few days before Christmas one year, and of course, we invited him into the house for a cup of tea.

Now, having children in the house we had a decorated, small gum tree as our Christmas tree in the lounge room complete with coloured presents strewn about under the branches.

Fred saw the tree and did not remark, but one could see him glancing over at the tree on quite frequent occasions.

Finally, just before he left, he could contain his curiosity no longer, and he said to Heather "What are you doing with the tree?" It appeared that he had never in his life seen or contemplated a Christmas Gum Tree.

Heather was then obliged to explain the whys and wherefores of the tree and how it related to one's beliefs, traditions, and a child's celebration of Christmas.

It came as quite a surprise to us that one could grow up to be a mature adult not having experienced the full celebration of Christmas as we knew it or its importance to a child's imaginings.

17

Christmas At Laura.

We were pleasantly surprised on our first Christmas morning at Laura.

We woke to the sound of gentle padding feet climbing the front stairs of the residence and then going down again.

During a short break in 'the visits', Heather and I peeked outside and saw several small Christmas-wrapped parcels, and by the time the 'visits' stopped, there were quite a few parcels that had been delivered.

Heather and I felt a little guilty in that we hadn't even thought of 'community presents' and here, although they could ill afford to do so, the indigenous population of the town had purchased/made these small gifts for our children.

Fortunately, we had a bulk supply of frozen chickens. We quickly thawed each of our supplies and cooked one chicken with trimmings for each family in the camp.

Laura Residence 1976.
Photo: Max Lewis

18

Ways and Means to Provide Meat to the Camp.

For the Laura Aboriginal population, the local general store was always adequate for their needs, however, there were times that they could not afford to purchase meat and they needed to hunt native animals to supplement their diet.

There was many a Sunday we would see George Musgrave taking his family out on a picnic, and always, he had his old .22 rifle to find whatever he could in the way of a wallaby or wild pig to shoot and bring home on his shoulders, and on occasions share with the rest of the camp.

I would, whenever time allowed, take George out and set a trap for wild pigs which would then be returned to the Police Station.

Wild pigs have a bad dietary habit in that they will eat almost anything including half-rotten meat and the like. Therefore, we fed the wild pigs a corn diet to rid them of the carrion in their gut, then butchered them for the camp.

One occasion, after someone reported the presence of a flying fox camp in the bush, I took a vehicle full of men out to the site who then set about either knocking down 'low hanging' foxes or shooting others, to gather a sugar bag full, then return to town where the camp set in to clean, cook and eat the meat.

Out of interest, I asked George if his wife could clean a few flying foxes for my family to taste. They were duly delivered, and Heather decided to stew them. Lucky we weren't ravenously hungry that evening, since they seemed to take forever to cook until tender. However once cooked, their taste was not unlike rich oxtail beef.

Peter Marriot, the Manager of Crocodile Station made it known to us that he was having trouble with a mob of half-wild pigs on his place. They had interbred with a few domestic pigs that had been left to fend for themselves around the homestead.

This mob was now hanging around one of his sheds where he had grain stored in a silo sitting at ground level, and which had been used to store a small portion of a sorghum crop from a season past.

The pigs had managed to access the silo through a loose side panel, and Peter had offered the pigs to us should we manage to trap them and load them onto a vehicle for transportation to Laura.

I had George build a pig sty from bush timber complete with an 'unloading ramp' at the top of the Police Station property.

He also built a loading ramp at Crocodile Station and rigged the loose silo panel into a 'trapdoor' that could be manually dropped into place once the pigs were inside the silo.

The day before 'D Day' I left George and a couple of young fellows to camp at Crocodile to guard the pig trap and drop the door at the appropriate time.

The next morning, the rest of the male aboriginal population of Laura travelled down in either the Police vehicle or the shop truck whose rear tray was enclosed in strong uprights and heavy wire netting.

We also took with us a couple of old fishing nets that I had previously confiscated but were never claimed by anyone.

On arrival, the truck reversed into the loading ramp with its low entrance point down in the silo where we had about 25 pigs trapped.

For safety's sake should we have any runaways, I had a good number of our group holding the fishing nets and semi-circling the area.

All it now needed was for someone to climb into the silo to hustle the pigs up the ramp and into the back of the truck. It was here that I ran into more than a slight degree of reluctance.

No swift talking worked, so to save face I felt it my duty to climb into the tank and do the job myself. I had identified the fact that there were no boars within the mob so felt reasonably OK.

I armed myself with a handy-sized length of 3x2 timber and jumped in. It started off quite well. The main mob immediately panicked and the bulk of them climbed the ramp. The only problem came from a half-grown sow that had a batch of larger piglets. She came at me with a roar and mouth wide agape ready to tear my leg off with her ugly teeth.

Luckily, I was able to hit the side of her face with a couple of blows with my trusty wooden weapon, which was enough for her and giving up, she too climbed the ramp into the truck. The only pig that was missing from our catch was a huge Large White domestic boar that Peter had borrowed to try to breed some 'quality' into the mob. Although quite tame, he was running loose, since he had not been in the silo when the trapdoor dropped, and Peter had asked us to take him as well as a temporary measure until his owner came to take him back.

Wild Pigs (Phootographer unknown)

Using our fishing nets, we attempted to get him tangled enough to manhandle him into the back of the truck, but try as we may, we only succeeded in stirring him up and he kept breaking the nets. Eventually, we were able to slow him down enough to wrestle him into the truck to be taken without further ado to the 'Laura Piggery'.

We were fortunate in being offered free maize by the Lakeland Downs Management, even the use of their corn cracker, and this is how the Murri camp was fed at Laura for a goodly period until the pork supply finally ran out.

19

A Novel Way to Catch Wild Pigs..

Bowie Gostelow's brother, Colin (RIP), once owned and operated Marina Plains Station, living there with his wife and young family.

In his day, Colin was a very athletic and able stockman.

Bowie told the story of Colin's exploits, aside from rough riding and bull catching on his property. Marina Plains, at the shoreline of Princess Charlotte Bay, was overrun with wild pigs, and to a degree, still is. Colin's 'trick' was to drive his Land Cruiser after a mob of pigs, pick the largest, and with his knife in his teeth, jump out of the open Toyota door, wrestle the pig to the ground and have the pig's throat cut before the dust settled. Before jumping, Colin would throw the Toyota out of gear, so that it would come naturally to a stop.

Marina Plains Station as the name suggests is situated on a flat, black soil, almost treeless plain where the risk of the vehicle colliding with a tree or running into a washout is extremely low.

Although, on one occasion he played his 'trick' with his young kids sitting in the back of the ute. Something caused the vehicle to veer to the left as Colin jumped. The vehicle rolled over. Somehow the children weren't injured, however, his eldest daughter ended up on the underside of the utility with her hair caught within the leaves of the rear springs and had to be removed from the predicament by having a 'haircut' using a pocketknife.

Pigs on the run (Photographer Unknown)

20

The Road To Dusty Death.

During my time at Laura, it was understood that I should travel to Coen each year to assist in policing the town during the weekend on which they held the annual Coen Races. George Musgrave, the Laura Tracker was never comfortable going to Coen since, coming from a different 'mob', was, in the past, made to feel uncomfortable by some of the Coen indigenes and he was therefore happy to keep an eye on the Laura township in my absence.

I would sleep in my swag in an area under the Coen Police residence occupied during those years by Sergt. Jim, his wife, and their family. Before my leaving Laura, I had been contacted by one of the station managers, to arrange for me to transport two Coen Aboriginal Ringers to Laura on my return.

The understanding was that they would both spend that night at Laura, and a vehicle from the cattle property would pick them up the next morning to take them to their destination.

The Coen Races again proved to be a success without creating too much work for the Police in attendance. As per the arrangements, the two ringers were waiting for me outside the Coen Police Station when it was time to return to Laura.

Although somewhat indeterminate, I guessed both their ages to be around 40 years, and both looked to be fit and well. We drove to Laura on a road that at that time could only be described as atrocious, but that was a cross that we all bore during those years before bitumen and/or regular road maintenance. But we stepped out of the Police vehicle safe and well if a little dusty and jaded.

I dropped the two men with their swags and other possessions off at the 'Laura Camp', the place where the local Aboriginal population lived before Government housing was built in the town. There they would make themselves comfortable and sleep in their swags until the next morning.

On my arrival at the Police residence, I noted that we had visitors from Townsville. Bill and Lorraine and their two girls had driven to Laura to spend a couple of days with us. We all had the evening meal together and then sorted the sleeping arrangements for our guests. As it happened the two girls would doss in with our kids, and Lorraine and Bill would sleep in a bed that we had set up on the side verandah immediately adjacent to Heather's and my bedroom. The rooms were divided by a set of double doors.

During the night, in fact, very early in the morning Heather and I (whose ears were attuned to hear such things) were awakened by the sound of the feet of George Musgrave climbing the front steps, and as we expected, said quietly, "You awake Boss?" I said, "Yes, George" and went out the front door to speak with him.

In his quaint way of speaking, he said, "One of them fullas you bring from Coen, he dead now". I questioned him as to what had occurred and all he could tell me was that he was awakened by the deceased's workmate, who told him that his friend appeared to have had a health attack and quickly became unconscious and died.

I asked George to arrange another place for the informant to sleep, and that I would take a moment to decide what to do with the dead body until morning when we would take it to Cooktown Hospital. I returned to the bedroom and discussed the possibilities of the best thing to do for now and was leaning towards placing the body in the watchhouse for the time being.

Our conversation seemed to suggest, "We'll bring the body up here". Unknown to us our guests had heard every word of our conversation.

Heather was concerned that we may have woken Lorraine and Bill and approached them from the rear rooms of the house. They were both sitting bolt upright, their eyes and mouths wide open in shock and they said to Heather, "You're not going to bring a dead body in here, are you?"

It took several minutes before we could settle them down sufficiently so that they might go back to sleep.

In the end, George and I wrapped the body fully into its swag and left it there for the rest of the night agreeing to load it before dawn and take it directly to Cooktown. (This is pre-body-bag days).

This we did, although it took more than a little effort to make it fit into the rear of the Short-Wheel-Base Toyota; after which we then left for Cooktown.

Doesn't it always happen? In the most inopportune circumstances, 'Murphy's Law' will decide to work and prevail, against man's best efforts, to try to make him look like a mug, rather than to our aspired professionalism.

As we approached Lakeland Downs just prior to daybreak we were flagged down by a couple of men who explained that their motor vehicle had broken down.

Have in mind that the SWB Toyota Land Cruiser has glass windows down both sides and across the back, making it easy to see inside, George and I were keenly aware that our deceased passenger, although covered, was in plain sight. Although he was not completely visible since on the rough road the body had slid forward until the head was now completely under my driver's seat.

Nevertheless, I was fervently hoping that the two men in the broken-down vehicle would keep looking forward as they spoke to us. As it happened, the men had repaired the problem with their vehicle and simply needed a push to start their engine, since they had run down the battery trying to restart it when it had stopped.

We gave them a push and sent them on their way, both parties greatly relieved but for two different reasons. We too set off to our destination, and in due course arrived at the Cooktown Hospital where we found the Doctor in Charge, Pat Hanush (RIP), waiting to take delivery of the body from us.

Former Cooktown Hospital
(Photographer unknown)

I reversed our vehicle until it was adjacent to the mortuary doors, and George and I wrestled with the body which now seemed to want to stay with our vehicle.

Finally, we had the deceased lying on the hospital stretcher which we then wheeled into the light inside the morgue where awaited the good Doctor. She had hardly even taken a cursory look at the body before she began to rage about its condition.

On top of the dirt and grime that the guy had picked up on the trip from Coen to Laura, as well as sleeping in his swag on the bare earth, followed by the transportation to Cooktown, the body was covered in dust and dirt. That was to say nothing of the nostrils which appeared to be full of fibrous dirt that they had picked up from 'sniffing' the underside of my seat over many the bumpy miles.

We eventually managed to persuade Doctor Pat that we had taken due care to get the body to Cooktown in as good a condition as the road and present circumstances would allow.

"Life was not meant to be easy" (somebody once said), and it sure isn't sometimes!

21

Some Palmerville Stories Not Recorded By History.

To Far North Queenslanders the Callaghan name is a well-known historic one that dates to the early years of the Palmer River Gold rush.

Two Callaghan brothers made their fortune by walking cattle to the goldfields and selling meat to the miners and their families.

The two brothers later took up country at Palmerville, and there laid the foundation for, and developed Palmerville Station. These two brothers married, and fathered children, and a generation later, another two Callaghan brothers owned and worked Palmerville.

One of these brothers married May Parsons (RIP), fathered his children, and then died relatively young, while his brother, Jim (RIP)., remained a bachelor.

In due course, the property was divided for each son. One son, Kevin (RIP)., whose property was distant from the original, named his property Fairlight.

The original Palmerville Station was then owned by the second son Micky (RIP)., and Mrs Callaghan's twin brothers, Alf, and Phil Parsons.

The original homestead block was split off from the property and became, aside from Mrs Callaghan's residence, the Post Office and weather station, which she managed. Jim Callaghan would remain to see out his days on the property.

Both Jim Callaghan (known locally simply as 'Callaghan') and the two Parsons brothers loved a cool drink on a hot day – and then some, to the degree that the three of them were alcoholics (although Phil in later years swore off it completely, to then become a sober man).

When drinking, whether by habit or out of malice – (nobody was ever sure,) the two Parsons used old Callaghan as a target for their jokes, something that Callaghan always took in his stride, provided that, at the time he was sober enough to remember what was done to him.

Each year just after Christmas, but before the wet season, the three men would ride from Palmerville to Laura leading pack horses to pick up their wet season supplies and return home.

While in Laura they would always camp in their swags on the concrete floor of the town Dance Hall which is conveniently situated next to the pub.

For the days they were in town, they would have a mammoth 'booze up' before returning home, and of course, while in town, Callaghan always bore the brunt of the twin's practical jokes.

The story goes that the three of them were quite under the weather and while standing at the bar, Alf and Phil, during the evening, took it in turns to walk behind Callaghan, pull up the tail of his shirt from the top of his trousers and rip it from tail to shoulder blade.

Callaghan said nothing, mooched over to the Dance Hall camp which housed the swags, and soon after returned to the bar, wearing another shirt, which, after a time would suffer the same fate.

This situation continued for some time until at last, Callaghan, wearing yet another shirt said: "Hey boys, knock it off. This is the last shirt I can find in either of your swags!"

oOo

The occasion was reported that the three of them were on the grog while sitting on the front lawn at Palmerville.

Mrs Callaghan upstairs had recently let her chooks out of their pen for a pick of green grass.

Callaghan, by far the oldest of the three men, finally choked down and was lying flat out on his back, well under the spell of a drunken sleep.

Seizing the opportunity, the Parsons boys caught a rooster and tied a length of string to its leg. The other end of the string, they tied around Callaghan's 'willie', which they had pulled out of his fly, and each time one of them emptied a beer can, he threw it at the rooster.

Mrs Callaghan, hearing unusual noises of alarm and pain emanating from the front lawn area, went to check, and was shocked to see a rooster jumping around, uttering an undignified cry of alarm, answered by Callaghan venting a cry due to the sudden pain in his nether region.

Of course, Alf and Phil suffered a somewhat more than gentle, loving rebuke from their older sister even though she, up to a certain level, had become somewhat accustomed to 'the terrible things they were always visiting upon poor old Callaghan'.

22

Call The Flying Midwife.

The Flying Doctor attended Laura several times assisting mothers with the birth of their children during our time in that town.

Although our Postmistress, Kay, had some experience in nursing, she was not trained in midwifery. She was very capable in her care, but we still required the presence of the Doctor to either evacuate the mother-to-be or deliver the baby in the mother's home.

On one memorable occasion, the pregnant lady was a young teenage girl who left it far too late for all concerned. The bedroom in which she lay was far from sterile, but Kay, the girl's mother, and all her sisters were in attendance while the Doctor was still in the air, travelling from Cairns.

I was in the police vehicle, speaking on the radio outside the house reporting the state of play to the Doctor and he was providing instructions.

Fortunately, he arrived in the nick of time. I picked him up at the airstrip and drove him to the house where he immediately cleared the room except for Kay and went about delivering the baby.

It was a difficult operation making do with what he had, although fortunately, the birth was a reasonably easy one. At one stage the doctor was sitting on the floor with his legs under the bed, assisting the birth.

Occasionally a birth would occur on the Flying Doctor aircraft.

One young girl was taken on the back of a 4WD utility, her minders having arranged for a half-way-meet with the Cooktown Ambulance which was heading towards Laura.

Quite interestingly, the baby was born on the back of the Toyota by torchlight before the halfway meet occurred.

Today there is a modern Aboriginal Health facility at Laura, staffed by one or two Nursing Sisters who, no doubt would be on hand to assist the 'new mums' of the future in such matters as childbirth and post-natal health.

23

A Favour For The Flying Doctor.

I was summoned to the Flying Doctor aeroplane before it departed from Laura. In other words, the Doctor had something of importance to tell me, minutes before he flew away carefree from Laura to Cairns.

On this occasion, he advised me that he had the intention of getting certain of the aboriginal women together to talk to them about something important. However, he had been distracted and overlooked the chore.

I said, "What is the subject matter, and can I do it for you in your absence?" I immediately regretted making the offer when he said: "I am arranging for the women to have IUDs (Intra Uterine Devices) inserted".

"They will have to be talked to about the procedure, explaining what will happen and the reasons why, and their permission obtained. They will then need to be transported to Cooktown Hospital to have the procedures carried out".

I thanked him profusely for giving me such a fantastic opportunity and set about getting the five women together to give them the good news and arranged to take them to Cooktown in a couple of days.

I conducted the presentation with the women all together to the tune of embarrassed giggles. (I too was embarrassed but withheld the giggles.)

We went to Cooktown on the appointed day, and I took them into the Hospital and waited for them like an expectant father until they emerged, all smiling. I then took them down to the main street of Cooktown for a cold drink before we hit the road back to Laura.

Here we were, all walking together in the main street while they told me in glorious detail what had happened and proudly told me, "And it was like you said, boss, it didn't hurt one bit".

I'm thinking to myself, "Man, that Flying Doctor owes me plenty!"

24

Scabies In The Camp.

The next time I was summoned, the Doctor told me that there was an outbreak of scabies in the camp and that immediate steps were to be taken. He gave me instructions as to what was to be done and advised that the Aboriginal Health Nurses would be there within a few days to take control of the situation. At the very least the medical requirement was for the affected people to have a very hot shower before an 'anti bug lotion' was applied, concentrating on the groin area. Simultaneously all of their clothes needed to be washed in boiling water, and anyone cohabitating with the affected person should receive similar treatment.

This meant that every man, woman, and child living in or around the aboriginal camp would need to be treated in this manner. Fortuitously, the Military was in the immediate area carrying out exercises and I needed to urgently tell their C.O. that should he have any men who were of the inclination to visit the camp at night-time, they needed to be aware of the scabies outbreak.

The Officer replied that not only would he convey this message to his men but further, he would direct that the clean-up of the camp would become part of their exercise, including the rigging of hot showers and laundry.

oOo

Now there were in town two brothers, of some indeterminate age but certainly on the top side of 60, who had made it their mission in life to be the camp 'sires' and had been going about this self-appointed profession with gusto over many years. Henry or Hank as he was known and Miles, in the dim distant past, had been the owners/operators of Dixie Station and were apparently the only male members present on the property, with an oversupply of dusky women carrying out the domestic chores.

The story goes that when they were first going out to Dixie, they had bought a Landrover utility in Cooktown but neither of them had ever driven a motor vehicle before.

They had the Landrover loaded to the gunnels with all their gear; saddles, quart-pots, flour drums, women, dogs, and had launched themselves west from Cooktown. On the first day, they hadn't reached what is now called Lakeland Downs, but they ran out of fuel just at dusk.

One of them set out on foot for the nearest property for fuel, while the rest set up camp. When speaking with someone at the property Miles or Hank complained that it was taking them a long, long time to get anywhere, and there was a severe lack of fuel economy.

Fortunately for them, he was speaking with someone who had nous and experience, and after asking several questions, the person came to the unbelievable conclusion that Henry, Miles, and Co. had driven in first (low) gear all day, not realising the vehicle had other gears that would drive them faster and more economically.

(Now, having now known that fact for many years, both men were still, in their 70s, driving the old Landrover in 2nd gear around town.)

The two men, having gone broke in the cattle venture through indolence and waste, moved to Laura and lived there for many years. Hank was now employed as the manager of the Laura Hotel, and Miles, general roustabout, and town layabout. Hank's one distinguishing feature, as he shuffled about in his bare feet serving clientele their liquor at the bar, was that he habitually hung his full false plate of teeth out his mouth and would only replace them into his mouth when he wished to speak, eat, or drink.

Miles apparently saw himself as a book of general knowledge and spent his time out in front of the hotel under the mango trees imparting his knowledge to all who would listen, while for illustration, he drew diagrams in the dusty earth with his bare big toe.

With age, their nightly forays into certain other people's bedrooms had slowed, but it seemed that a game was continually being played out by the male Indigenous Australians whereby there was a morning's competition as to whether one of them had been visiting.

Donkey Camp Heater similar to that rigged by Military at Laura Camp for bathing and laundry purposes.
Photographer Unknown

There was always the honour of being the one who found footprints that, whether it be out of modesty, or attempted trickery, approached the camp, always from a different angle. George Musgrave took great delight in reporting to me "Ole Hank came visiting last night. He come from down da road ober dere".

What has this to do with the scabies outbreak you ask?

Well, there was understandably a certain amount of resistance to the prescribed course of action to counter the outbreak, and despite the Aboriginal Health Nurses' best efforts, it was becoming progressively more difficult to get the tailenders to undergo the hot shower and apply the lotion.

By chance, one day, Miles was overheard to be yawping to anyone who would listen that this scabies stuff was all a furphy, and these bloody Government people should go back to town and leave these Laura-ites alone. Hearing of this, I now had a sense of where the resistance was coming from, and where the indigenous people were going for 'white man counsel'.

I called Henry and Miles together and gave them the good news that they both were going to have a hot shower and receive a dose of the lotion since it was common knowledge that they were cohabitating with certain members of the camp, and should they refuse, I would personally put them in the shower and apply the lotion; that I would brook no argument as the subject was closed. That story quickly spread around the camp, and the Nurses had no further problems. Hank and Miles enjoyed a hot shower of their own volition. I am yet to find out if, in fact, they used the lotion. Nevertheless, scabies disappeared from the town.

I'm still enormously thankful that I didn't have to apply the lotion to Hank and Miles.

25

C'm 'Ere Boss, I'll Make Y're Day.

I had gone out to the shed late at night to turn off a generator. A large truck was standing near to the shed as it had done for some time, awaiting repairs before it might be pressed into service in our future Rodeo Yard building project.

I came out after turning off the generator and in the darkness, I thought I heard a noise, but with the sounds of the diesel engine still ringing in my ears, I couldn't identify its source.

It happened again and this time I heard a female voice whispering "Max, Max". Long story short, Topsy (RIP). was hiding under the truck waiting patiently to 'make my day'.

My first reaction was to give her a good tongue lashing, but then I thought if I upset her, she'll go back to the camp and say that it had happened with the boss, so I spoke to her in a kindly manner and sent her on her way.

There was never anything said or heard about the incident, which, by the way, Heather thought was hilarious, and Topsy is yet to 'make my day'.

Others of my colleagues who've served at Laura in more recent times tell some quite hair-raising stories of Topsy willingly making a lot of people's days but that is a story or more for another day and for someone else to tell.

oOo

26

An Ancient Mariner – Three Times Lucky On The High Seas.

Our nearest neighbour at Laura was an old Scotsman named Scotty Divers (RIP). He would no doubt have had a more normal Christian name, but I have either forgotten what it was or more likely I have never heard it.

Scotty had a colourful past. He was a seaman in the Royal Navy during WWII and was 'locked in the brig' on numerous occasions for drunkenness. On three separate occasions, ships on which he was serving, were sunk by enemy fire, each time losing many of his mates.

He jumped ship when visiting Fremantle, West Australia, and disappeared, and has remained in Australia ever since.

He worked his way north, and finally settled at Laura to become a bore driller, operating Southern Cross percussion drilling rigs.

These worked on the principle of constantly 'dropping' a heavy steel cutter down a hole, chipping away the bottom, not unlike a giant crowbar, into the underlying rock to finally have a borehole which he then lined with a steel bore casing.

Scotty was, as they say, deaf as a post, but as deaf as Scotty was, it was said that his ears were finely attuned to the thump of the boring tool striking at the bottom of the borehole.

Regardless of his condition, be he sober, blind drunk, or whatever, should the borer change its 'tune' indicating that it needed to be advanced deeper down the hole, he would identify the sound and stagger to the bore-head and make the adjustments. He did this in rain, hail, sunshine, day, or night.

Scotty, when we knew him, had largely retired from boring and he and his Land Rover ute were contracted to the Cook Shire to do road patching and maintenance.

Another job for which Scotty quoted on and won was the fencing around the Police property at Laura an area of about 10 acres. To assist in this project no doubt with the agreement of my predecessor Herb, he hired George Musgrave, thus contributing somewhat to George's income. The result was an excellent barbed wire fence surrounding the whole property.

Whereas Scotty used to cut across the police property to walk to town, he was now effectively shut out of his usual path.

Scotty was the carrier of many bush yarns drawn from his years spent on cattle properties, and from the many hours spent drinking with the likes of Bowie and Miles Gostelow, Alf and Phil Parsons, and the like.

One story Scotty told was of a time he was 'out bush' sinking a borehole when he was bitten on his bald head by a red-back spider.

His immediate feeling was that this was a death sentence to him, not necessarily because of the bite, since the bite is not normally fatal, but because of the position, right on top of his head, of course quite close to his brain.

He knocked off for the day as the pain from the bite grew, and no doubt, if he had liquor in his camp, he would have had a few drinks. He then lay down on his swag never expecting to rise again. He said that he put in a bad night from the pain, but then slept for the next day and night, to then discover that he wasn't dead.

He recommenced his work and survived the ordeal completely. The bite area was sore for a day or so, and the pain then disappeared.

Scotty, for the most part, was a teetotaller, drinking Coca-Cola at the pub, but on occasions, I estimate about once every nine months, he would break out on alcohol, his chosen drink being Bundy rum.

His exploits during his sessions made for many interesting times, affecting the whole town, with Scotty staggering around the pub, verbally abusing everyone he knew until he fell into the horrors and imagined all kinds of creatures following him around.

On one occasion, he told us during his sober, story-telling sessions, that the Quinkan man was following him around, and Scotty was petrified as to what the Quinkan might do to him.

There were a few 'out of town' ringers camped on the floor of the Dance Hall, with their swags side by side. Scotty had to be with people, so, after the pub closed, he pushed his way to lie in between two ringers in their swags.

He said these guys were both very drunk and arguing almost all night, even to the extent of throwing punches at each other across him, however, he refused to move, fearing that the Quinkan was waiting outside the hall.

Whenever Scotty was sober, he would drive his Land Rover utility from his house to town. But when drunk, he would attempt the walk across the police property, climbing through the barbed wire fence.

One night I heard cries coming from the direction of the Watchhouse. I had no prisoners locked up, so I needed to go and investigate.

Here was Scotty, hung up in the barbed wire he had tried to climb through about four hours before and had been hung up ever since. He was, of course, very drunk.

Within Scotty's list of attributes was that of storytelling and he could relate a bush yarn in his broad Scottish brogue along with the best of them.

oOo

He told a story of Bowie Gostelow and his family – one of the many that seemed to be about or include Bowie.

It went as follows...

Bowie owned a large red gravel tipper truck, (this truck was used in the building of the rodeo yards.)

Bowie, and his wife and their children were travelling in the red truck from Laura to Coen for the annual Coen Race weekend, with Bowie driving, his wife in the passenger seat, and the kids in the rear tipper tray.

Just north of Musgrave is the Bamboo Range, as steep, and rough a piece of road you would find anywhere during the 1960s.

The truck was struggling up the range, and Bowie was busy with his gears and everything else that demanded his attention. During the pressure of the moment, Bowie mistakenly and unknowingly pulled the hydraulic hoist lever, lifting the rear tray and emptying his kids onto the roadway.

Fortunately, due to the condition of the road, the truck was travelling very slowly and none of the children were injured, but being dressed to go to the races, they would all need a good clean-up once they arrived at Coen.

Bowie, arriving at the top of the range realised that the tray was in the raised position and there was no sign of the kids. Worriedly they waited at the top of the hill until their family eventually appeared one by one, walking up the roadway towards them.

oOo

Among Bowie's brothers, he had one more, this one was called Matthew (RIP), (or Matt.) Matt was travelling with a mate in a Landrover, both two sheets to the wind, and Matt's mate was driving.

At some stage, the driver lost control of the vehicle and it rolled over, throwing Matt's mate to the roadway. Matt stayed in the vehicle for the wild ride, and was completely uninjured, although his mate was lying on the road unconscious but otherwise unhurt.

Matt interpreted the incident as a personal affront to himself caused by his mate. So he climbed from the wrecked Landrover, and, walked up to where his mate was lying on the roadway. Verbally foretelling the immediate future held for his unconscious compatriot, without so much as a quick inspection for broken bones or other injuries, hurled not only his abuse but fists and boots for the short time his temper lasted unassuaged.

Once the unconscious man awoke and came to his senses, they found a bottle somewhere, toasted the happenings with another drink or two, and remained the best of friends.

oOo

Old guys like Scotty, Bowie, Matt and Miles Gostellow, Alf and Phil Parsons are the kinds of people who add spice to the bush towns.

In their own way, while at times being a darned nuisance by their drunken antics, are, during their more sober times, hardworking men with great life and work experience. When they die, they are sorely missed by all and sundry for their often overlooked fine qualities.

27

"Proper Lady Missus."

At Laura, Heather had quite a lot to do with the Aboriginal women, whether because of a busted head, or through helping young mums feed their children, and through those kinds of interactions, she was well known by them.

On occasions, when I was absent from town, she would have to escort drunk women (who went willingly) to the Watchhouse, and it seemed that at that time the sober women asked for this to happen and agreed with her actions.

On one occasion she was called down to the Camp, again in my absence, when one of their number, Ivy was drunk and quite violent to all those present.

Heather attended and spoke to Ivy knowing full well that Ivy was well past doing as she was asked and willingly locking herself up. As if to emphasize the point, Ivy picked up a large stick, having lost her temper, and trembling with rage as she threatened Heather.

Immediately the group of women surrounded Heather and said "You stay away, Hivy! this is proper lady missus, and you can't hit her", and they stuck by Heather, surrounding her until Ivy eventually calmed down.

Aside: The name has stuck with Heather and to this day occasionally you may hear one of our family affectionately call her "Proper Lady Missus".

oOo

28

Birthing Pains Of The Laura Rodeo.

I was attending one of the Laura Race meetings doing my thing as a member of the policing contingent, reflecting I must say on several things, since race meetings, from a policing point of view, are fairly tame affairs.

It is only after the races finish and the solid drinking commences that a Police Officer earns his or her wages.

My reflections were principally in two directions:

1. But for my uniform, I wouldn't ordinarily be attending a race meeting. I wasn't brought up that way, and being neither a gambler nor drinker of alcohol, I had little interest in what was happening: and
2. I felt for the kids, the aborigines, and others who had little funds with which to neither wager nor drink.

Also, here we were in the middle of cattle and horse country, and there were no appropriate entertainment amenities. There was nothing other than race-horse riding, in which ringers and station people were permitted to strut their stuff, that had anything to do with their work skills.

I mean, here was a racecourse facility packed with people of all walks of life and all ages. There was undoubtedly a certain percentage of youngish local people with a hankering to get into the cattle industry, learn to ride, learn to handle cattle, and the rest.

There was nothing that was aimed at encouraging would-be recruits to the industry, and I felt, well, we were missing a golden opportunity.

Two days of witnessing gambling and boozing, and the third day recovering to drive home-what were we doing for our younger people?

The obvious answer to the problem lay in a germ of an idea for a rodeo. The trouble was that the 'greenhorn' that was mulling over the problem was only a few years out of the city himself and almost totally devoid of any ideas about how to start or run one.

Also, what would the Laura Racing Association say to my even suggesting an alteration of their revered facility to accommodate rodeo yards and arena?

I discussed the idea with Heather, and we carried the thoughts around with us for some time.

At some stage, I mentioned the idea to my mate Bill. Bill started thinking and spoke words of encouragement but was almost as lost as I was as to how we could put such a plan into action.

Somewhat fortuitously perhaps, the Lakefield Station manager, Ron Teece (RIP), drove into town and up to the Police Station. After dealing with whatever Police matter, he had, I mentioned the idea to him. The more I outlined, the brighter his eyes became. He said that this was the very thing that he had been thinking about during the few years he had been working in the Laura area.

In fact, he already had some self-designed and drawn plans for rodeo yards and the arena, which he would be happy to supply to us should we go ahead with the project.

One more difficulty was foreseen by all of us, and that was where could we find enough available flat land to place rodeo grounds and a car park.

We spoke to some members of the race society about sharing their facility and received a very cold shoulder indeed from them. On top of that they would in no way support the idea of a rodeo since to stage such an event on the Sunday immediately after the races Friday and Saturday would "rob the races of crowd size".

Someone raised the question as to how large the Sports Reserve upon which the racecourse was built, and to our surprise, we found that the reserve was well over three times the size of the racecourse, and it included a sizeable, circular piece of flat country semi-surrounded by a natural 'Amphitheatre'.

This was exactly what we needed for our project.

The Cook Shire Council members were very supportive of our cause and not only granted permission to use a portion of the reserve but supplied their surveyor to peg the site to enable us to grade and shape it to make it perfectly level.

We had well-attended meetings for the project where I was encouraged and cajoled into becoming President of the Building Committee.

This was to organise working bees, using whoever was available from town and nearby stations, as well as raising money to pay for the project.

And so, the year 1976 became our construction year to hold our first rodeo on the Sunday of Race Weekend 1977. The idea meant, in effect, constructing rodeo yards, an arena, and facilities as well as organising a rodeo event, all within less than 12 months.

- I could now see the wisdom of their electing me as the President, since I lived in town possessing some authority,

I could better arrange working bees on weekends, leaving the qualified 'rodeo people' free to organise the future event.
- We were loaned chainsaws and trucks to cart timber.
- Terry Struckel, then of Killarney Station had a medium size sawmill on his property, allowing him to offer to cut and donate sawn timber for gates and other building constructions.
- Other property owners granted access to stands of timber that we could cut and use for posts and rails.
- Bowie Gostelow had a large tipper truck (the same one described earlier from which Bowie had tipped his kids onto the Bamboo Range Road) currently located at Fairlight Station which he offered for our use if we were prepared to drive out and pick it up, some 50 kilometres.

Bill and I drove out there one afternoon and found that the truck had suffered some damage to the front right mudguard and grill but seemed otherwise driveable.

I climbed into the truck, started it, and set out for Laura. I quickly found out how rough it was to drive, and it was when I applied the brakes that I identified that they were somewhat dicey, making it necessary for me to drive the vehicle slowly.

We were approximately 10k out of Laura, climbing a small pinch in low gear, when I felt something in the gearbox let go and the gears stuck in neutral.

The brakes would not hold me from travelling backwards, and I swung the truck in a large circle off the side of the road until it came to a stop.

Fortunately, there were no washouts in the immediately surrounding country. We needed to tow the truck to Bowie's house at Fairview, only a short distance from where the incident had occurred, and there we left it until we bought a small fulcrum pin to replace the broken one in the gearbox.

On a later occasion, we had another attempt to bring the truck to Laura. This time I had a few of the Murri lads riding in the back of the truck. All went well until we reached the northern crossing of the Laura River which has a steep downward approach to the crossing.

As we neared this downward slope, I attempted to change to a lower gear to assist the brakes in slowing us down but found that the truck cab had shifted on its rusty mounts due to the rough road, and I was unable to select any gear, which meant the truck gathered speed as it went down the hill.

The group of Murries in the rear of the truck all jumped off, leaving George Musgrave and me to ride the truck to whatever was going to happen. Fortunately, nothing untoward occurred. The truck gathered speed, ran across the river crossing, and climbed the other side.

Once we delivered the truck to Laura, there it stayed in the Police yard awaiting further repairs.

A portion of the original Yards awaiting the first
Rodeo at Laura 1977
Photo: Max Lewis

Our rodeo grounds project continued to progress as people became available for working bees, and station people gave us time at the yards whenever they were passing through, or when they came to town on business. Little by little our project came together.

On the big day of the rodeo, I was at the grounds at daylight, and already some riders were there warming up their mounts, preparing themselves for the first event of the day, the Camp draft.

I felt relieved that I was alone in the police vehicle because it allowed me to give vent to my emotions and felt proud that our year's work had paid off and here in front of me was the evidence, and people were now taking advantage of our hard labours, according to plan.

There were several firsts during that day, not the least that the local aboriginal population, mainly the males, had the opportunity to ride and take up the challenge they certainly did.

People were expressly warned that nobody under the influence of liquor would be permitted to ride or compete. The young bucks all respected this decree and held off drinking at least until they had finished competing.

Heather, never one to shy away from a challenge, issued her own. This was aimed at the station ladies.

She told them that she had organised for a ladies calf ride, or in her language, 'a Ladies Micky Bull ride' and that she would compete if they did.

The event was held and Heather, true to her word, had her ride, competing against the very considerable riding skills of the station ladies.

The day progressed well, having been efficiently organised by Ron Teece and his team. When the end of the day arrived, and the awards were handed out we could then breathe a sigh of relief for a project well completed.

I was transferred at the end of that year but remained confident that the Laura Rodeo would continue, and indeed it has. The reins were picked up by the members (and in-law members) of the Raymond family of Kimba Station and others to develop it into the success story we now witness this year in 2022.

The Rodeo is still held on the Race weekend, now very much part of the fabric of Laura's events calendar going from strength to strength.

We returned to Laura for the 20th anniversary of the first rodeo, and I was very much humbled and honoured in learning that the Rodeo Grounds were being named 'The Max Lewis Rodeo Grounds'.

Who would have imagined what the humble 1977 beginnings could have lead to? Photo: Max Lewis.

Forming up prior to Campdraft, Rodeo 1997. (Photo: Heather Lewis).

From rough beginnings to a fully functional and modern style venue attracting crowds to the activities and the town. Congratulations to all succeeding Committees
Current Photos courtousy of Laura Rodeo and Campdraft Asssociation.

29

Managing The Heebee Jeebies.

It's intriguing how superstition can, it seems, cloud the mind and reasoning of people of all or any social or ethnic standing.

It is my experience that Australian Aborigines, and some indigenous peoples from other countries, can be more susceptible to the work of 'spirit people' than the average white European.

They also seem to be more prone to be affected by bad luck omens and the like, perhaps because, living closer to nature they are looking around their natural surroundings for the 'higher power' or the work thereof.

I, along with other Police Officers who had the good fortune of working with George Musgrave (RIP) hold the greatest respect for his bush wisdom and the talent he applied to his work as a Police Tracker.

As talented as George was, he perhaps surprisingly was as likely as any of his kin to be spooked and lose all sensibility and reason should the circumstances of the moment so dictate. Circumstances like when the Kadiji Man or the Quinkan come to visit.

More of George in a moment, since I must offer another tale that will illustrate my point.

At Camooweal in 1967, I was sent to Avon Downs, just a few miles over the Northern Territory border. At that time there was a Police Station by the highway, unaccompanied by houses or shops - just a Police Station standing alone beside the road.

Harry Wilson was the name of the Police Officer stationed there and he had reported to Sergeant Don at Camooweal that an Aboriginal woman had turned up out of nowhere. She said she was sick and needed transportation to the nearest hospital. I have no idea why Harry couldn't have driven to Camooweal, but there I was at Avon Downs to ferry the woman to town.

I saw that she was accompanied by a male Murri, and he gestured that he wished to speak to me in private.
He said, "I want to tell you something boss."
I said, "What do you want to say?"
He said, "She bin sung boss."

I had no idea what he meant and looked at Harry for a translation. Harry told me that the woman's husband had accused her of being loose with her sexual favours and he had gone to their 'spirit man' for 'advice' as to what he should do.

The spirit man had cursed the woman and told the husband that the problem was fixed. The woman not then knowing of the curse had almost immediately fallen ill, and now, here she was, looking for help.

We travelled to Camooweal, and I left her with the Sister at the Hospital. The woman was examined by the Nursing Sister, and the next day by the Flying Doctor, but neither could find anything wrong.

Two nights later she died in her sleep. I often wondered just what the Doctor would have put on her Certificate as to the Cause of Death.

Be that as it may, her body was transported to wherever she came from and buried, - no further questions asked...

oOo

Eight years later, at Laura, two people turned up from Edward River. Husband and wife, their names were George and Bertha Lowdown.

They stayed locally for a time because George had work at one of the Laura area properties. When the job was finished, George left for Edward River, but Bertha stayed on at Laura.

By and by Bertha was sporting a new boyfriend in the person of Arthur Sellars. They cohabitated for some months, as happy as two 45 (thereabouts) year-old lovers could be.

One night, the aboriginal quarter of the town was in absolute turmoil.

Women were screaming, men yelling, and George Musgrave was quickly over at the Police Station waking us to say that George Lowdown and a group of men were over at the 'camp' and they were looking to kill Arthur Sellars. I quickly went with George and searched for the men, but apparently, the men had gone.

There were three very responsible and well-educated young women living in the town, two of whom were related to most of the aboriginal people in the town, but each had been fathered by a white man.

They were very well-adjusted young women who worked at the Hotel.

During the time of the camp 'troubles', they were caught up in a superstitious panic, and right or wrong they wanted to spend the nights at the police residence with Heather and me.

We could not see value in going along with this request, although it was plain to see that the girls were terrified.

We finally arranged for them to stay with another young couple, who at the time managed the Laura Café, which is approximately 1 km out of town, on the main road.

The 'camp panic attack' reoccurred shortly after, at a time when I was out of town and Heather was called upon by George Musgrave to act as the 'Sergeant' because they had Lowdown trapped and surrounded in one of the houses.

Heather was caught in the moment and felt as apprehensive as any other member of the crowd but put on a brave face and made sure that George, whose knees were quaking, stayed with her, although the thing he refused to do was to enter the house first.

She had him open the door to a bedroom and again she had to take the lead. This room was where it was alleged Lowdown was 'trapped' but on inspection, they could see that the room was empty. George said, "He must have gone out the window Missus."

After I arrived home a day or so later, I questioned George as to what had happened and he told me that Lowdown and crew had returned and terrorised the camp again, and this time he had the Quinkan man with him.

George said, "We found where he bin camping while he here". I said, "Is he still here, or has he gone?" He said, "No, No, he still here boss I show you the place."

We went down to the 'old camp' where the Laura Murries had lived before the Government Housing settled them in town, but where an old hut remained.

"The Quinkan Man" As depicted in the Quinkan Gallery, Laura
Photo: Max Lewis.

George put his finger to his lips and we both went around to the doorway only to find the hut empty. There were some half-fresh footprints in the dust outside the hut and I said, "Whose footprints are those, George?" To which he replied, "That's him, that George Lowdown's!"

We returned to town. I dropped George off at his house and immediately went to find Tommy George (brother of George Musgrave) and asked him to take a drive with me.

Down at the hut, I took Tommy to the doorway and said, "Whose footprints are those, Tommy?" Tommy took one look at the footprints and immediately said, "That's old Arthur Sellars, boss." I said, "Are you sure, Tommy"?

He said, "Yair that's him, boss, I wouldn't make a mistake on that one".

I contacted the Police at Edward River and they confirmed that George Lowdown was indeed present at Edward River (now called Pormpuraaw).

Soon after that, I sat George down and asked him just what he had based his decisions on as to who or what was disturbing the camp. He finally admitted that he had overreacted after the whole camp suffered some kind of 'camp panic' that seemed to overtake the whole group, and someone had surmised that it was George Lowdown.

I said to George Musgrave. "You are going to talk to the whole camp and tell them that all this nonsense is finished and there will be no more night panics over George Lowdown."

He did so, and the night terror incidents ceased.

30

^%$#@~&%$* @ (Alias Bill Jackson.)

I have a good mate: I have known him for some 48 years. We first met him, his wife, and his daughter when we arrived at Laura in 1974. He introduced himself as Bill and told me that he drove the truck for the local store and Post Office and that his wife, Kay was the Post Mistress.

Bill and I hit it off immediately and as alluded to above, we are still good friends, but more of that later.

I learned that Bill's parents were Polish and had migrated to Australia towards the end of the Second World War. They lived on a farm at Kaban on the Atherton Tablelands, Bill having received his education at the Ravenshoe School.

At some time during an information-sharing conversation over coffee, Bill revealed to me that his true name was Zdislaw Jaszczyszyn.

He explained to me that he has, over the years struggled to present his wondrous moniker in a way that is acceptable and understood by those he dealt with both informally and formerly where the spelling of a name is more important, and then, dealing with Aussies who have a bad habit of dubbing others with nicknames.

While he was working in Central Queensland in the coalfields he somehow or other eventually became known by the unlikely title of 'B.J.' or if you like, Beejay.

This nickname kind of stuck, to the extent that Bill had the title added to the front of his work shirts.

Now step forward to his arrival at Laura and he began driving the shop truck for the Laura Store. One of the people he came to meet was Bill Jackson the owner of Wolverton Station north of Coen. Someone meanwhile had taken note of Bill's nickname and noted that it also represented Bill Jackson's initials.

Somehow or other Beejay began to be called Bill Jackson, and that name also stuck so that voila! we have another Bill Jackson on Cape York Peninsula.

Bill wore the name because it was easier to go with the flow than to argue against it, especially when the only thing he had to offer in return was Zdislaw Jaszczyszyn.

So, by chance, this Bill Jackson became the driver of the truck for the Laura Store, and presto! he was now being called Bill by everyone who knew no different.

Came the time when, driving his truck in Cairns, picking up shop supplies, it became late, necessitating turning on his headlights.

Soon after, he was stopped by the Police, who indicated to him that his number plate light was not working.

One thing led to another, and Bill was asked to present his Drivers License. It was then that he found that he did not have the license, and he, therefore, requested that he be permitted to present it to the Police Station at Laura when he returned home.

The Police asked him to identify himself, to which he replied "Bill Jackson".

It was as he was later driving home to Laura that Bill realised that he might be going to be in serious trouble with the Police, having accidentally given a false name to the Police in Cairns.

Bill approached the Laura Police Station downhearted and full of remorse to tell his tale of woe because the name he had given to the Police did not match the official handle indicated on his license.

It was, of course relatively easy to explain on paper how the problem had occurred, and of course, the compelling evidence was the presence of the name Zdislaw Jaszczyszyn there for all to see on his Drivers License.

Subsequently, all passed quite happily, and he was issued with a Defective Vehicle notice. He was also directed to present his truck to the Laura Police Station once the defect was repaired.

The explanation I gave on his behalf was duly passed to the 'Powers that Be' in Cairns and Bill heard no more about the matter.

The years went by and our respective paths went in other directions, although both families kept in touch informally, and even met from time to time. My transfer path brought us to Ravenshoe and Atherton.

Bill and Kay also came and moved to and from the Tablelands.

After I retired from the Police Service in 1999, we lived for several years in Townsville, and in 2006 my health circumstances demanded that we find cooler air.

Consequently, we returned to the Atherton Tablelands, purchasing our present home at Yungaburra.

Having agreed to purchase this home, I found myself talking to the Real Estate Agent, a person well known to me from my policing days in Atherton.

He said to me "Do you remember Kay and Bill?"

I said, "Of course."

He said, "They own the house right next to the one you've bought!"

Fate had kindly brought us together again to continue our friendship now in retirement.

I still call my mate 'Bill' and I rarely ever use his surname. Our strong friendship remains while we grow old, as good neighbours, talking about the weather from the 'vantage point of the seats of our rider mowers, and comparing notes about our latest gammy elbow, gouted foot, or arthritic neck.

31

Power To The People.

Although we had been aware of the fact before our arrival, it still came as quite a shock that there was no 240-volt electricity, and no town water supply connected to the Police residence at Laura.

There was however a 32-volt lighting plant.

Ancient Southern Cross Diesel Milking Machine engine connected to a 240-volt generator similar that used at Laura Residence 1976.
Photographer Unknown

I later assembled my own generating plant, purchasing a 3kva generator and driving it with an old single cylinder milking plant engine that I had bought locally from Bowie Gostelow.

It served us well until we left when I sold it to one of the station owners.

During the week we left on transfer a beautiful remote starting 240-volt generating plant large enough to power the whole township was installed at the Police Station. The 32-volt lighting plant was retained during the night hours when the 240-volt unit was not in use.

Laura Police Residence 1997
Photo: Heather Lewis

32

Mrs Holzheimer Goes for a Drive.

Of course, one of the bugbears endured by people of that time (the 1960s/70s) were the roads, and that prevails today in centres further north on Cape York.

Both Laura and Cooktown are now well served with a bitumen road from Cairns. In the early 1970s, the bitumen road ended just north of Mount Molloy, and drivers faced hour upon hour of rough, atrocious roadway that takes a ghastly toll on motor vehicles.

Those mostly affected by the road conditions were the transport operators, and there were several of them, but no doubt the most memorable among them was Holzheimer's Transport, running from Cairns to Weipa and all points in between.

Memorable because the chief driver doing that trek regularly was none other than Toots Holzheimer (RIP), a wife and mother who happened to love driving trucks. She was a legend in her lifetime. She could work all day, doing every bit of toil that any man could, and she did it for years.

On occasions, during school holidays she would take her children with her in the truck, and the kids, having been brought up tough lived that life on the road helping where necessary in loading and unloading.

My two young nephews came to visit us at Laura from down south during the school holidays. We were driving north near Musgrave and came across Toots Holzheimer, broken down beside the road.

She had a couple of kids with her, and I stopped to check on her. We found her and the kids sitting under the semi-trailer, out of the sun, and all eating ice cream with their hands all scooping it out of a '1 gallon' plastic ice cream tub. My nephews couldn't believe what they were seeing.

oOo

On another trip north, Toots pulled up at one of the local Company Stations with a semitrailer load of fuel in 44-gallon drums for the station and found the station manager's wife the only person there.

Toots unloaded the fuel, manhandling each heavy drum with apparent ease, and when she finished, she was filthy from dust and spilled diesel, so much so the station manager's wife offered her the use of the shower to clean up. Toots, true to form, said, "Nah mate, she'll be right, can I use your hose?"

To the astonishment of the manager's wife, she shushed herself all over with water from the hose and, soaking wet, jumped into the cab of the truck and dashed off, headed back to Cairns. The manager's wife could only stand and watch, simply amazed.

Toots, one time was greeted at the Cairns Airport by someone who knew her but almost missed the recognition because they had never seen her dressed up. She was more often than not in her rough working gear.

Toots' airport friend was curious as to why she could be travelling in this fashion and asked her where she was headed.

The reply they received was typical of Toots Holzheimer, "Oh I'm just flying to Sydney to get me a new MAN", and away she went.

Toots' favourite brand of truck was MAN, and one of the trucks displayed at the Winton Museum is one of Toots' last trucks she drove before her untimely death.

Toots was tragically killed in a wharf accident at Weipa in the early nineties, getting caught between a suspended, swinging heavy load and a solid, non-budging object.

She remains one of the great popular characters of the Peninsula roads, stations, and towns.

Toots was certainly a legend and continues to be sorely missed by all who are fortunate to have known her.

Memorial to Toots Holzheimer erected at Archer River Crossing, Cape York Peninsular.
Photographer unknown

33

Sunny Coast/Green Grass Eumundi.

We transferred out of Laura towards the end of 1977 and drove to our new posting at Eumundi, immediately inland from the northern Sunshine Coast. Sharee had already started school and Brendon was to commence Pre-school.

After having left Townsville as babies, they had grown some but were virtual bush kids, who would now learn a new way of life, not quite living in the 'city', but experiencing life closer to amenities and larger volumes of people.

One moment stands out when relating to our children discovering what most take for granted.

We were driving somewhere at night and the kids discovered the urban streetlights.

They both broke out in excited chatter saying, "Look! They have lights in the streets just so that you can see the houses."

My duties changed to accommodate more structured patrols, traffic enforcement, and greater interaction with Police colleagues since we had Cooroy Station to the north, and Nambour to the south by only a few kilometres.

Running north to south through the Eumundi Division was undoubtedly some of the best quality highway roadways in Queensland at that time. Both a blessing and a curse, the Bruce Highway saw traffic pass through at 100kph day and night.

I was to learn that this self-same road can also, regularly witness many horrific traffic accidents as bad as any occurring throughout Australia.

34

What's In A Name?

Moving from the bush to Eumundi meant that I always had fellow police officers within reach should I require assistance. I immediately noticed the difference in having two police at Cooroy, only a few kilometres distance, and then a little further away was my 'District Office' station at Nambour with a larger number of police officers.

The working relationship with these other police officers was always cordial, however, I did notice a certain reluctance to form a closer friendship among certain of the police at Nambour, which, although it never affected our joint efforts within our police work, did raise its head from time to time. It was a small problem, but the cause or source of the issue continued to avoid me.

The answer came from the most unlikely direction.

The Eumundi station was a CPS establishment, and one of the responsibilities was a light one involving the SGIO (State Government Insurance Office) which would later become Suncorp. Our involvement was mostly to do with issuing third-party insurance when a motor vehicle was registered.

The SGIO representative used to call monthly to collect any money and the related paperwork. In doing this, the representative had the opportunity to be involved with a broad section of police officers from around the district.

He and I carried out what work we had to do, and on this occasion, he stayed for morning tea. During morning tea, the subject of the relationship with certain of the Nambour Police came up, and surprised, he said, "Don't you know?" I told him that I had no idea.

He said, "Well, a few of the Senior Constables at Nambour believed that they had a fairly good chance of being appointed to Eumundi, and when it was announced that you had it, the word was that you were a relative of Police Commissioner Terry Lewis, and that's how you were appointed to Eumundi.

I laughed and said to him, well first, I'm no relation to the Commissioner, and secondly, I was appointed here because I have just completed three years in a remote bush station, and the Department has openly said that it will look after remote police in terms of their next appointment under these circumstances.

I think that you can go back and have some fun with the Nambour Police by telling them that I really am a cousin of the Commissioner and that I have been placed here to keep an eye on them.

I am pleased to say that my relationship with certain members of Nambour Station improved drastically once the truth of the matter was known.

oOo

Soon after we arrived in Eumundi we became involved with the School P&C. This group was very active in money raising and held licensed cabarets on regular occasions.

To do this, the group needed to keep quite a large supply of liquor, bought at a cheaper price when bought in larger bulk lots. The problem was where to store the supplies.

It became known that the local Policeman was a teetotaller, and had a double cell watchhouse that was rarely used. That being so, it fell to reasoning that there was one cell that was never used, and quite possibly its use could be diverted to solve the liquor storage problem, and in fact, this is what eventually did happen.

One morning I was working in my office, and, looking out the window I saw a male person walking up the police yard, crossing into the 'residential' part of the property.

I went out to him, catching him up from behind. I asked him if I could help him, and when he turned to face me I recognised the face of the Police Commissioner, Terry Lewis.

My mind commenced madly questioning the reasons why he was there, and of course, 'was it because he had heard about the stored liquor in the watchhouse'?

I commenced walking with the Commissioner, passing by the watchhouse (thankfully) and made our way all around the house.

Mr Lewis finally explained that he was passing by and realised that he had never seen Eumundi station and would therefore use this opportunity to do so. Without even coming inside the station, or talking about operational matters, he climbed back into his car and drove away.

Even today, I am at a loss as to what that visit was all about. Maybe it was to stir my 'guilty conscience' over the liquor.

I don't think I will ever find the answer to that question.

35

An Unshakable Family Code.

I attended a road accident one evening on the Bruce Highway just outside of town, the driver had lost control of his vehicle and rolled the car over.

The driver, a young man, was uninjured, and as is the normal routine I gave him a roadside test for alcohol that proved to be positive.

I had of course already asked him his name and address in Brisbane, and I noted that his surname was the same as that of a work colleague of mine.

While driving the young man to Nambour Police Station for a breathalyzer test, I inquired whether he had a connection to my workmate of the same surname, to which he replied, "Yes, he is my older brother."

On our arrival at Nambour Station, he was duly tested and charged, and then set free on bail. By that time, it was about 9 pm. I said to him, "Would you like to use the phone to get a ride home?"

He said, "Thanks, I'll ring John (my colleague) and get him to come up and drive me home".

He made his phone call. The call lasted about the time it would take to tell his story, and he hung up and said, "John's too busy at work to come".

I suggested that he ring the other members of his family, and he progressively made a few calls.

He finally came to where I was waiting and said, "Looks like I bloody walk home".

The last I saw of him he was walking out to the highway to thumb a lift back to Brisbane.

I learned later that the family had an extremely strict code about the use and misuse of alcohol, and it was this….

Should someone in the family have been drinking and get into trouble over it, no other member of the family would under any circumstance assist him or her. The code in this case was followed to the letter.

I recently posted this story on social media, and little did I predict before doing so the angst and division it would foster.

Opinions abounded from both sides of an argument, one, supporting the code adhered to by the members of the family in refusing assistance to the young man, and the other, strongly scathing, alleged that the young man was put at significant risk, forcing him to find whatever other means to return to Brisbane from Nambour.

I offered neither opinion nor advice in the argument, but my memory harked back only a few short years prior, to a time when as a single young man I was thumbing a lift from Brisbane to Kalbah to meet up with a 'love interest' and then return home by the same method.

In doing so there was never any consideration that I was in any kind of danger while thumbing a lift.

Of course, the 1960s and the '70s were a different age and in today's environment I too would hesitate to do some of those things that we were free to do back then.

36

A Trauma Shared In One Small Community.

I previously mentioned good roads and serious road accidents on the highway passing through Eumundi Division.

One such accident occurred around 11 pm one evening, involving three motor vehicles. One, travelling south contained a woman driver with her two young children.

The driver lost control at a slight kink in the road direction, slewing it into the path of another vehicle travelling in the opposite direction.

This car contained a couple who were returning home after attending their retirement function in Nambour.

The two vehicles, locked together, were then struck from behind by a third vehicle containing a woman driver who had been to Nambour to bring home several older children who had been to see a movie.

In all, eight people were killed in that one accident, which to that date was the worst accident in Australia in terms of the human toll. Tragically that grim record has since been surpassed many times in other parts of the country.

To make the accident worse from a community point of view, all involved were local Eumundi district people apart from those in the first mentioned vehicle, who came from an area only a few kilometres north of Eumundi.

There were two Constables sent to the site by Nambour Police. These were young men who were just coming out of their Police Traineeships.

One Police Officer was plainly about to break down emotionally, and I thought it prudent to send him back to my Police Station for the requisites I needed for this scale of a road incident.

On his arrival, he fully broke down in front of Heather, to the degree that she needed to sit him down and give him a drink of tea thus giving him the time to compose himself.

I learned later that the personnel working for the funeral director who transported the deceased persons to the Nambour Hospital were also highly emotional over the circumstances.

That both Police and all others present were so affected would tend to indicate that it could well have caused a serious problem for others involved in the incident.

Because none of the deceased people were yet identified I had left instructions that none were to be undressed at the mortuary, to assist in the identification of the deceased by the use of clothing.

Upon my arrival hours later at the morgue, all bodies had been undressed and laid out wherever one could find room. Fortunately, all were later identified without difficulty.

At the scene of the incident, work went on measuring, taking note of wheel skid marks and all other indicators that may be used as evidence in a future Coroner's Court inquiry which would be investigating the cause and circumstances surrounding the deaths.

Our work took us until daylight, and the crashed vehicles were removed from the scene. Thankfully, we could now reopen the road to traffic.

For Police working the scene, the horror of these types of tragedies is revisited while ever the investigation of the incident continues.

- There is the trauma shared with members of the family as they are taken into the mortuary to have their beloved family member identified.
- Each body is subjected to a post-mortem examination attended by a Police Officer, usually the Investigating Officer.
- Members of next of kin are naturally wishing to learn the circumstances of the accident, and normally there is more than one grieving person present.
- The fact that most people involved in this incident were local and in a rural area, other locals were curious and wished to talk about the incident.
- In the case of this accident, the husband of the driver, who initially lost control of her vehicle, lost not only his wife but also two children. He was traumatised to the degree that he was visiting the police residence every other evening in tears, seeking some relief from his grief.
- Due to the circumstances and the time of year, Heather and I travelled to the above person's home (at the request of a close relative) and removed all the gifts from inside which were awaiting the arrival of Christmas.
- Heather and I knew one of the other children who died in the accident, - I have known that family since my childhood.
- The trauma is revisited many, many months after the incident when the police evidence is dealt with by a Coronial Hearing.

The above road accident details are revealed, not for shock value, nor to stir morbid curiosity but to illustrate the fact that Police Officers are required to not only participate, but take the lead action in many traumatic happenings.

To do so often leads to some Officers eventually suffering from such problems as Post Traumatic Stress Disorder. (PTSD)

In my case, although the sight of, or dealing with death has never particularly worried me, it was because of the seriousness of the many accidents occurring on that highway, and dealing with the traumatised living in the after-events that I chose to eventually transfer away to guard against a similar fate such as this occurring in my own life.

37

Bulldust, Crocs, and Salt Pan.
- Burketown.

In 1980, after serving approximately two and a half years at Eumundi we decided that I had experienced enough highway traumas, and now it was time to consider promotion.

I applied and later received notice that I was to be promoted to Sergeant and transferred to Burketown at the bottom of the Gulf of Carpentaria.

Our transfer to Burketown in 1980 was a time for some changes in our mode of travel, and we decided to exchange our sedan motor vehicle for a 2.W.D. Ford F100 ute, because we were towing a 16 ft. caravan, and our children, ever-growing, needed a little more legroom while travelling.

We, therefore, had a fibreglass canopy installed and fitted therein a car seat and their own individual 'sound systems'.

The departing was, in a way a little upsetting, since we were leaving many friends whom I had known almost all of my life. On the other hand, the idea of moving away from the road trauma was a refreshing thought. Nevertheless, the need for change prevailed even though our stay at Eumundi had also been rewarding and fulfilling.

Before our departure, we had a visit from a guy who had spent some time around the Gulf of Carpentaria. He provided us with some background information, some useable, some otherwise.

One statement he made in addition to showing us some photographs, was about crocodiles in the rivers. This had a profound effect on Brendon who at his age was quite impressionable, as we were to later find out.

Reaching Cloncurry and the turnoff north towards Burketown, we made a detour to Mount Isa.

I intended to introduce myself to my new District Inspector since it made sense to do that now rather than commence work at Burketown and then immediately return to meet my new boss.

Doing so turned out to be fortuitous since out of a conversation about the transportation of our furniture from the railhead to Burketown by road, we learned that the job had been given to the owner of the 'Mail Truck' whose only transport vehicle was an open deck semi-trailer. (Really, not very kind to our piano and other furnishings.) This arrangement was quickly remedied, and we travelled the rest of the way to Burketown.

Early the next morning, Brendon, who was now six years of age, had been quietly holding onto a piece of information he had learned at Eumundi and was seen to be acting unusually.

He had interpreted that there were hordes of saltwater crocodiles at Burketown and he was checking out all points outside of the house through all the windows, looking for the salties in our yard.

We did ultimately see plenty of crocodiles, both saltwater and fresh, but thankfully not in town.

Steve, the man who was to be my permanent workmate and destined to eventually become a good friend, was on leave and absent from the Station.

He was being relieved by Bob, a Constable from Mount Isa.

38

A Small Piece Of Japan.

One of the enduring memories that remind us of our time in Burketown will be that of a very old indigenous lady who lived there within her race but who was appreciated by all who were fortunate enough to know her, irrespective of their colour.

Her name? Well, she was known simply as 'Granny Gooch' (RIP). She was recognised by that name by everyone.

Spin back some 70 years, when the world was at war and Australia, having participated, doing its part in Europe, was now in partnership with the Americans desperately fighting to keep the Japanese out of the Pacific, Torres Strait, and Australia itself.

Indeed, bombs had been dropped on Australian soil at Darwin and elsewhere, and enemy aircraft were skulking in Oz skies regularly.

So, something like this brought a Japanese aeroplane into the vicinity of the Gulf of Carpentaria. The aircraft had been damaged, or perhaps it was simply out of fuel since it was in its last throes of life before crash landing into the 'Carpentaria seas', but not before a solitary figure floated from the stricken machine with a parachute.

The man, now swimming in the water struck for the south, where he was aware lay the closest land. He finally made it to the shore where he found extensive boggy sand flats and the odd scrawny mangrove. Continuing to travel south he found harder but desolate black soil, and eventually came to the township of Burketown.

Being an enemy pilot, he no doubt sought to avoid whatever white people he saw, but he was eventually discovered by the local aboriginals who provided him food, shelter, and hospitality.

It wasn't long before he became comfortable with these people, and, perhaps due to his darker complexion he was overlooked by any white person, thinking he was a mixed-race Indigenous Australian.

As time went by, he noticed and was noticed by a young aboriginal girl. A friendship developed, and as these things often do, the couple fell in love. This of course led to marriage and meant that the aboriginal girl's surname now became Yamaguchi.

Burketown's 'word of mouth history book' fails to tell what happened from then on, other than that Mr. Yamaguchi stayed on in Burketown at least until the end of the war.

There is no record of what happened to him after the war, whether he returned to Japan, or whether he stayed on and eventually died and was buried in Burketown.

Granny Gooch survived and was living in Burketown during our term there.

Granny took a particular liking for my workmate Steve, and on occasions when she had any on hand, would give him a treat of sand goanna tail-the best part of the goanna, having less grease in the meat than other parts of the animal.

As alluded to above, Granny Gooch was liked and appreciated by everyone who took the time to get to know her, and without any effort on her part, continued to create enduring, sweet memories of Burketown.

39

A Lockup Can Be A Thirsty Place!

Gregory Downs Township, south of Burketown once had a Police Station of its own until the 1960s when the facility was sold, but the buildings were still there.

Gregory Downs has its own Annual Racing carnival, as well as other events at other times requiring a police presence.

The problem of the arrest of prisoners arises from time to time since Burketown is an hour's drive away from Gregory, time that police officers may not be able to afford should trouble be ensuing at some public event requiring their immediate attention.

Some enterprising Police Officer had arranged for a large log to be placed outside the old Police Station and set it up so that a prisoner could be secured to it by handcuffs.

This worked well for a time but came the day a large Yugoslav was locked up.

With the Police out and about, the man and log disappeared.

The Police immediately mounted a search and eventually found him at the bar of the Gregory Hotel, sipping a beer with the log balanced on his shoulder.

40

How D'Ya Like Y'r Chicken - Hot or Cold?

At different times, depending on the availability of marketable fish there would be several fishermen working out of Burketown, net fishing in the nearby salt water.

They came in two types:

First, there would be the boat fishermen, perhaps living at Burketown, or living on their boats, but using Burketown as a base, and then there would be the 'land planters' who worked out of a riverside camp and took out and set their nets in the nearby rivers.

The land planters would associate more commonly with the people living in town, and it was through this association that we met Ras.

Now Ras was always looking for ways to do a deal that would make his living on the river camp more comfortable or easier.

Heather had an arrangement whereby she would cook a fruit cake and exchange it for a fish or two from Ras.

Heather's problem was that she could never maintain the egg supply in sufficient numbers from the laying hens she had, and her fruit cake recipe called for quite a few of them.

Discussing the matter with Ras, he offered to bring a good number of chooks from his home in Townsville, and he would pick some up on his next trip to unload his latest freezer load of fish meat. Heather of course agreed to the arrangement.

In due course, Ras left in his ute, loaded up with his large freezer box full of fish, saying that he'd be back in a week. True to his word, Ras returned to Burketown within the week with his large freezer box carrying around a dozen laying hens, and these were soon unloaded and introduced to the few hens that we already had.

Ras told us the following story:

He'd left Townsville, after having put the hens into the freezer box, which, being otherwise empty and the inside temperature somewhat like the air outside. It was a long way to Burketown, it was high summer, and as he drove, the thought of his roadside 'watering holes' was ever on his mind, since he enjoyed the odd cold beer on a hot day. Ras has his favourite watering holes along the way to Burketown, so he pulled up at the pub in Quamby at about midday and climbing out of his ute, he thought to check on the welfare of the chooks and found them quite hot and panting. He thought 'while I'm here I'll run the freezer to cool them down, and that is what he did.

It does sometimes happen that a man gets hung up by the tongue when he visits the occasional pub, and of course, this is what happened to Ras. , but once free of the pub and drawing closer to his ute, he suddenly remembered the chooks.
'

"Enough eggs to keep up with a recipe for my rich fruit cake" Photographer unknown.

Quickly turning off the freezer motor, he opened the box, fearing the worst.

Looking down into the freezer box, here were the poor chickens, huddled together in one mass of birds, attempting to keep warm, but still alive.

Ras feeling somewhat guilty then drove the rest of the way to Burketown without visiting another 'Watering Hole' but every so often stopped to check on the welfare of his birds.

Burketown was a welcome sight for Ras as it came into view, and he couldn't wait to unload the hens at Heather's place to free himself from the heavy responsibility.

Whether it was the treacherous ride suffered by the hens from Townsville to Burketown, or something else is not known, but whatever it was, it sure spoke to those chooks in the right manner, because they were the best layers we have ever had, easily keeping up with the demands of the cake recipes.

41

There Are Other Places Besides Toilet Seats To Set Up Shop.

Burketown Police Watchhouse 1983
Photo: Max Lewis

We managed to be introduced to one of the lesser expected hazards of Burketown.

One which certainly is rarely identified by those advising of the hidden dangers in the area...

We arrived at Burketown not all that long after a sparkling new watchhouse had been built to house the errant members of that metropolis.

Reddbaack Spider. (Photographer Unknown).

When sweeping out the building one morning we noticed that literally dozens of spider webs had been built, overnight. The spiders were everywhere.

On our closer examination of the inhabitants of the webs, I discovered that the spiders were all redbacks.

It took some quick action on all official sides to purchase and transport an appropriate insecticide to spray onto the walls to be rid of them before one of our 'clients' managed to be bitten.

42

A Mite More Than A Belly Ache.

It is not particularly surprising in a small Police Station for a man to 'drop his pants' or show some other part of his anatomy to a police officer in the privacy of the police station to get an opinion on some malady or other and ask for advice as to what action he should take.

Usually, country hospitals are staffed totally by females or a female Nursing Sister on her own, and the said male is a little shy about baring himself to her. The Police Officer seems to be the accepted way to get around the problem, except now it is not all that rare for the Police Station to be also staffed by a female, but that's an altogether different story.

A young man arrived at the Burketown Police Station complaining that he had a sore on his stomach and asked me to have a look at it.

I immediately saw that the front of his shirt was wet, and once he had shed his shirt, there was a suppurating messy wound, oozing matter, smelling horrible with redness all around it, and it took no medical degree to see that it was badly infected.

He said, that the reason he was here supposedly having the wound 'checked' was that his drinking mates at the pub no longer wanted to sit near to him because 'he stank'.

I told him to put his shirt back on and I would drive him to the hospital, which I did and left him in the care of the Nursing Sister.

It wasn't all that long after that the Sister telephoned to say that the mess was almost certainly a Sexually Transmitted Disease and a particularly nasty one at that. Highly transmissible to others, which meant that the young man's clothing had to be immediately destroyed by fire.

I had asked the young fellow where he was staying since he was normally a resident of Doomadgee. He told me and further explained that the lady of the house was his sister.

I attended his sister's house and explained the situation to her asking if I could see his bedroom. She took me through the house, and on entering the bedroom I could see that he was sharing the room with his sister's young children, and to make matters worse, there was clothing strewn about the floor, both his and the young children's.

I immediately felt sorry for the young woman when I explained to her what the Nurse had said - that all clothing had to be destroyed, knowing that she would have been unable to replace the kids' things without causing herself financial hardship.

She told me that by chance, she had a wood-burning copper and that she could boil all of the clothes in there if that would suffice.

I knew that she was a reliable young woman and that she would do as she said, and so, after checking with the Nursing Sister, I told her to go ahead but not to touch any of the clothing with her hands, and boil wash them is what she did.

It has been my experience that STDs are a serious problem to control for the Aboriginal Health authorities, since many Murries are extremely coy about talking about problems 'down there,' and it is as difficult for Police to get a handle on who to be careful of when making an arrest and the like.

My workmate Steve was put into the unenviable position one time when it became necessary for him to give mouth-to-mouth resuscitation to a young bloke at Burketown, and while it was happening the guy vomited into Steve's mouth.

This all happened outside of the Hospital where the young guy was waiting to see the Sister because he was feeling unwell and was later diagnosed as having an STD.

Fortunately, Steve suffered no ill effects from the episode.

43

Two Burketown Brothers.

Burketown had its version of 'two brothers of note' in the form of Don (RIP) and Logan (RIP).

These two were married; Logan's children were grown up and gone, while Don's were a little younger and still living at home. Don was a Shire Councillor, and Logan 'ran' the family business which seemed to comprise running a few head of cattle on the town common.

Logan had suffered a kick to the head by a beast some years before our arrival at Burketown which left him seriously 'unpredictable' and liable to do weird things from time to time.

Logan and his wife lived immediately opposite the Police residence, and we were privy to some of Logan's strange behaviour from time to time.

For instance, we awoke one morning to some unusual noise emanating from 'over the road' at daylight. Upon investigation we espied Logan standing on the peak of his roof, cracking his stock-whip and yelling at the top of his voice. What had seized him at that moment was difficult to judge.

On another occasion, a crowd of people of all walks was present at the Gregory Races, and during the 'lull' between race events, Logan, at the time was 'two sheets to the wind' with alcohol. Garbed in his hat, jeans and high-heeled riding boots, he had set up a high jump 'rail' with ropes and was competing against himself attempting high jumps in front of all to see.

With nothing said to deter him, he kept up the jumping it seemed for half the afternoon.

Members of the watching race crowd, most of them knowing Logan, simply paid no attention to him. In the end, when he stopped, he was so filthy from falling onto the dusty ground, that one was unable to judge the true colour of his shirt.

oOo

Burketown is bordered by Armraynald Station on its southern side, and we had been suspicious for some time that Logan was illegally killing the occasional Armraynald beast for beef.

Being reasonably close (give or take 100–200km) to the Northern Territory border means that occasionally a wild buffalo would stray over the border and arrive in the vicinity of Burketown.

Steve and I had the permission of the Manager of Armraynald Station to shoot and kill any buffalo that came onto their property. There was great excitement among the local Murries one afternoon since a buffalo had been seen close to Burketown.

We loaded the SWB Toyota up with murri men and butchering gear and soon found the beast wandering across an Armraynald paddock. Steve's .308 rifle quickly dispatched the buffalo after which the butchering commenced right there and then on the ground.

We had not gotten very far with our butchering when we heard, and then saw, Logan's Toyota Utility making its way across the paddock to pass by us within about 200 metres.

We saw Logan turn his head and look at us but he continued on his way until he was out of sight.

It wasn't long after, we heard a rifle shot from the direction in which Logan had disappeared, and Steve and I were left in a quandary as to what we should do...

Do we investigate the gunshot and allow the buffalo meat to spoil on the ground, or ignore Logan, get the meat back to town for the good of the Murries, and catch up with Logan later?

In the end, we elected to do the latter, and there was much grand rejoicing amongst the Burketown murri citizens that evening.

The following morning, Heather and I heard a vehicle with a diesel motor come driving through the laneway between the Police Station and the residence.

It was Logan with a whole side of beef, for us should we need any fresh meat.

It was a sly ploy on his part to implicate us in his nefarious activities of the evening before.

I had to bite my tongue from telling him any more than, 'No, we are OK for beef now'.

44

A Touch of Yellow Fever.

In the mid-1850's graziers in the Carpentaria area had difficulty selling their beef due to the distance from the markets.

In 1866 a beef boiling down works producing tallow was built at what we now know as Burketown for the purpose of processing the local beef. The works had its ups and downs, including a fire and other negative factors that led to the closure of the works in 1877 leaving a rusting hulk to deteriorate ever since.

Today, all that is left is a heap of rusty machinery, but recently there was movement afoot to do something to make the site more attractive and memorable to tourists.

When we were in Burketown in the early to mid-1980s little was known by the town-folk of Burketown, and the general belief was that the site had been a meat canning factory during the world wars for the purpose of pressing tins of bully beef for the fighting forces.

How do I know that it existed? Well, my workmate Steve and I had our fingers lightly rapped after we took a huge cast iron press plate from what was left in the rubble and converted it into the heaviest and the best B.B.Q. plate you would find anywhere installing it in the back yard of the Police residence.

We were able to enjoy just one B.B.Q. with it before the Shire Council took it back because of its reputed historical value. Local history has it that the meatworks was officially deliberately destroyed by fire when it (unjustly) received the blame for introducing and perpetuating "yellow fever" among the good people of Burketown and the nearby Indigenous Settlement of Doomadgee.

The truth of it was that hepatitis is, and some would say has always been prevalent in the Burketown/Doomadgee area. The scourge visited the Burketown Police Station in 1981 and I was laid low for a couple of weeks with Hepatitis A.

It just so happened that at that very time the Burke Council was converting the town to sewerage and there was a handful of Council workmen digging and busting up (with a jackhammer, picks, and shovels) our square concrete septic tank.

That was until we advised them of my diagnosis resulting in an immediate cessation of work in our yard.

After my recovery - it seems like some 6 weeks afterwards, the disease had one final kick.

We were on holidays and heading south with our F100 ute towing our caravan.

By the time we were approaching Augathella, I was starting to feel more than a little light-headed and sick. We pulled into the town, which was a little way off the Highway, to fuel up the truck. I was standing beside the open left side door, guiding the petrol nozzle into the fuel filler spout when I caught a whiff of fuel vapour and immediately began to sway on my feet.

Fortunately, Heather was there beside me and she was able to give me support as I rid myself of the fuel nozzle, and climbed into the passenger seat while Heather drove to the Augathella Hospital where I was admitted for observation.

Meanwhile, Heather and the kids had to get the rig out of the hospital yard and find a place to park in the township until I was released from the hospital.

Now Heather felt far from confident driving the truck and van, particularly when it came to reversing the combination. She had seen two old guys sitting together on the verandah, and overheard one say to the other "Watch this, this'll be good".

Hearing the old dudes and seeing them watching made her even more determined to do a perfect reverse manoeuvre, which, full marks to her, she achieved and drove the rig away.

The Hospital Matron had advised Heather that there was no caravan park in the town, and the only thing available was a truck stop out on the main road. So, she found and parked the rig at the truck lay-by accompanied by two apprehensive kids.

The Matron in the meantime had discovered that I was a Police Officer and decided to ring the local Police Sergeant and explain the situation.

As a result, he drove up, spoke to Heather, and offered her a corner of the Police Station yard to spend the next day or two under the protection of the local 'Constabulary's wing'.

All's well that ends well and I spent a couple of days in the hospital, fighting an 'all over the body' itch and pharynx infection.

Once I'd recovered sufficiently, they released me to then continue our journey with instructions to spend a required recuperation week in Charleville before travelling onwards to our destination.

45

Claude The Kiwi Mechanic.

Having come from New Zealand, Claude, an excellent mechanic, took up a job working with others on a fishing boat in the Gulf of Carpentaria, based at Escott Station just outside of Burketown. Claude later left the boat, and, having a builder mate, a Swiss guy by the name of Martin, but more commonly known locally as Mushgang, – Claude had him erect a steel shed right next to the Police Station

Claude commenced business as the local mechanic, an enterprise that still exists to this day, and over the years Claude has been the Burketown Mayor and has energetically participated in civic goings on since he set up shop there in about 1982. In fact, Claude had the honour of representing his Country at an Anzac Day ceremony once a fishing boat in the Gulf of Carpentaria, based at Escott Station just outside of Burketown. Claude later left the boat, and, having a builder mate, a Swiss guy by the name of Martin, but more commonly known locally as Mushgang, – Claude had him erect a steel shed right next to the Police Station

held at Burketown.

We had noticed that there seemed never to have been such a ceremony held there each year, and so, with the involvement of the schoolteachers, we had the school kids march to the music of a Salvation Army band, played over a cassette player from the back of a ute.

Claude laid a wreath at the foot of an Australian flag, and the same was done by a couple of school kids representing Australia.

I played the Last Post on my trumpet and one of the School Teachers gave the Anzac Day address. Never let it be said that Burketown fails to hold its end up when it comes to Anzac Day recognition– and multi-cultural too.

At the risk of shocking the lady readers of these lines, I need to advise that the widely used nickname that Claude was given by the wags around town was 'Claude Balls'!

Why? "Well,", it is said "that was what he received when he attempted to copulate with a wild, unromantic lioness" (clawed balls)," said those who dubbed him with the title.

There was a very workable arrangement that we Police organised with Claude to counter a shonky practice that was being operated by a motor car wrecker in Mount Isa. At that time, a vehicle owner was not required by law to provide a Roadworthiness Certificate within the Burke Shire, and the Mount Isa wrecker was selling bomb cars to the Doomadgee Murries.

They were paying for a 'Permit to Shift an Unregistered Vehicle' for the vehicle to get them to Burketown where the customers were expected to go to the Police Station to buy their Vehicle Registration. He did OK for a little while until we awoke to what was happening with the motor cars breaking down regularly while travelling the hundreds of kilometres from Mount Isa to Doomadgee. We developed our own system requiring a letter from a qualified Mechanic certifying that the motor vehicle was safe to be on the road before we agreed to register their motor vehicle.

Thereafter, once some proud new owner of a mechanical car wreck had to also immediately pay extra for the new pride and joy to be repaired, people started to avoid the cheap market at Mount Isa. Claude's garage work multiplied manifold (although this was not the aim of our arrangement over the non-registration of faulty cars), and the unfair practice of the Mount Isa wrecker was effectively nipped in the bud.

MAX LEWIS

Kiwi (Public Domain)

46

A Murderer Visits Doomadgee.

During, but towards the end of the time that I was laid low with Hepatitis, Sergeant Dave, who had been sent from Mount Isa to relieve at the station during my illness, came to the police residence and said, "Max, I'm afraid we have a problem."

I asked what the problem was, and he explained that the residents of Doomadgee were talking about a visiting Murri from an Aboriginal Centre up north on the Peninsula who had arrived at Doomadgee and that he was supposed to be in prison for murder.

Dave had checked and found that an indigenous man by the same name had indeed been charged with murder. He had subsequently been sent to a secure hospital for the criminally insane, and now, after about 6 months, on the advice of the medical authorities, he had been adjudged to be 'cured' and released into the community.

A rider over his release was that he remained within the confines of his aboriginal community, supposedly the one where he had committed the original crime.

Dave told me that he and Constable John (RIP) were going to go to Doomadgee to speak with the man, and he was offering me the chance to go with them in case of trouble, be it physical or procedural.

Dave had a warrant for the arrest of the person, and also instructions from our District Officer that we should interview him before arrest, and should he offer any objection whatsoever - **"Any objection whatsoever!"** he should be immediately arrested.

The three of us travelled to Doomadgee and asked one of the residents the whereabouts of this person.

We went to the house pointed out and found our man out in the yard with an axe in his hands, chopping wood. The man was huge, (as in tall and full of muscles).

We felt that we should approach him from three different directions, and, having reached our respective starting positions, we began to walk towards him.

The man spotted me first and stopped chopping the wood.

We continued to approach him as I spoke to him and asked him his name.

He told me and the name matched the paperwork on him. I kept my distance but continued talking until Dave and John reached him and took the axe from his hands.

We asked him where he was from, and whether he wished to return to his community.

With a shake of his head, he said, "No", which was the objection we needed, and we arrested him and returned with him to Burketown.

Dave and John escorted the prisoner to Mount Isa where he was further dealt with by the police there. At no time was he violent towards us, for which we were extremely thankful.

47

An Attempt to Satisfy an Old Bird's Fetishes.

George's country cousin showing off his 'right hook'.
Photographer Unknown

Burketown had its own pet emu in 1982 (as does Camooweal), walking around the streets quite happily and free. His name was George.

George used to have a female mate that had died, leaving him to endure the loneliness of 'widowerhood.'

One might almost die of fright if walking along a Burketown street at night, to be softly bumped in the back and suddenly see George's head looking over your shoulder.

George habitually tried to 'hump' tractor or grader tyres attempting to allay his natural urges.

It was no real surprise the day I was opening the Police mail to find a collection of tire brochures sent by a tourist to George as 'emu porn'.

48

The Grand Political Event That Doomadgee Put On The Map.

The following story is of something that actually occurred at Doomadgee in the early 80s and has been told and retold ever since by many of those who witnessed the event. The grand occasion was announced wherein some puffed-up politician was on his way to visit Doomadgee Aboriginal Settlement to do something or other that politicians do. The place was spruced up and everybody was garbed in their best clobber for this 'Number One highlight of the year' type person to grace them with his presence.

The aeroplane arrived, and amongst the fluff and fanfare of plovers, cockatoos, galahs (both types), and other attending souls, the Queen's great and glorious representative was ushered before such curious subjects and their dogs who were interested enough to attend, plus those required by state protocol to be there.

As politicians are wont to do, 'His Onlyness' desired to appear culturally aware, thereby earning the ultimate prize of a greater share of the spoils when votes are divvied up on Election Day. In the presence of such a literal 'pantheon' of cultural diversity, he, therefore, did what he considered to be the most appropriate. Walking into a clearing out in the sun, with a quick defensive scan of the gathering for the odd angry man with a spear or 'gonny knocker', he sat down on the dusty ground to 'pow-wow' with the locals in the manner he believed to be the most familiar and acceptable. The locals, ill at ease due to the grossly naive spectacle, looked at one another, shuffled their bare feet in the dust, and said, "What dis stupid bugger doin' sittin' on da ground inna 'ot sun? We not 'sittin' out 'dere' an 'pickin' up sunburn! What 'e thinkin' we silly buggers like 'im?"

After having sat out there in the sun with his 'advisors' for what appeared to be an inordinate period, the great man finally realised the error of his ways, came to his senses, stood up, and returned to the welcome shade, no doubt feeling severely self-conscious as he finally allowed the proceedings to commence. The half-smile of embarrassment remained on his face for the rest of the ceremony until he could at last escape to the relative seclusion of his aeroplane seat and leave that dastardly place behind.

That day, friends, history was made. A pollie actually learned something he would never forget, but on the other hand, would never speak of again. So much for a 'grand political event'. Never let it be said that our politicians are not culturally aware.

Four Wheel Drive splashes its way along the main road from Burketown to Doomadgee 1983
Photo: Heather Lewis.

49

The Great Burketown School Fire.

During our time there, Burketown was fortunate enough to have a fairly keen, active SES group comprised of locals (mainly Shire Council workers) who worked together every working day and met from time to time to train for their SES duties.

My workmate and I had a desire to see just how an effective team the group was since it appeared that the only time they formally activated was whenever a cyclone was threatening in the Gulf of Carpentaria.

On top of that, the hierarchy at the SES was largely the same people who were the 'lower-level management' of the Shire Council, placed at a certain level in the Group for their standing in the Council, rather, it seemed, than their capacity for organization within the Group.

We formed a group of our own comprising the two Burketown Police Officers, and their wives, the Hospital Sister, the School Principal, and the Electrical Power Station Engineer. We created a scenario utilizing the School's covered playground as a 'second-floor' venue.

The scenario was that a motor vehicle had collided with the school during night classes for children and adults, causing the building to partially collapse, causing a fire in the classroom, as well as fallen wires thus causing an electrical hazard. The only set of steps to the 'classroom' had collapsed. The exercise was set at a given time on a Saturday afternoon, and the SES group would open an envelope giving them the details of the emergency.

We had strung ropes around the 'room' to represent live wires. We had a good supply of 'victim/play actors' who had varying injuries and conditions including a frantic woman trying to climb the ladder the SES had erected at the scene, a 'drunk' trying to 'help', and incapacitated victims who required evacuation from the 'upper floor'. In all, the exercise tested the group, and without rancour, demonstrated any failings the group had, along with their good points. One SES participant reported that "It felt so real, the hairs were standing up on the back of me neck."

Mostly though, the afternoon was a great success for Police/Public Relations, finishing the exercise with a friendly barbeque.

50

Grand Ole Granny Dawson (RIP).

We travelled from Burketown to Ravenshoe in 1983, and in so doing, strengthened and confirmed our previously held love of the Atherton Tablelands.

The Police Station was, at that time a two-officer station, and my workmate throughout my time there was Senior Constable Ric.

Not long after my arrival, I received a call from a local who lived about 10klm from Ravenshoe on a run-down, non-operational dairy farm.

The caller proved to be an old Lady of 90 plus years, wearing a nineteenth-century style long dress with a long-sleeve white blouse which was fastened at the throat with some kind of badge that, on later, closer inspection I recognised to be a silver-coloured Salvation Army badge.

This old lady introduced herself as Mrs Winifred Dawson, better known by the folks of Ravenshoe, and indeed everywhere else, as 'Granny Dawson'.

If Granny's clothing was severely dated, so too were her speech and mannerisms. I told her my name was Max Lewis, but I was immediately instructed that she intended to refer to me as 'Sergeant Lewis', end of story.

Her house was built from pit-sawn timber, clad with weatherboards and a corrugated iron roof. The house had electricity installed, but only one power point (in the laundry) and one or two electric lights.

The powerpoint was used to heat water for her clothes washing with an old-fashioned 'handheld' submersible heater standing in a large bucket, and all other hot water came from her wood stove.

Granny Dawson welcomed me to the area telling me that she was aware that I was a member of The Salvation Army. She too was a member but no longer attended the church due to her age, and she no longer owned a motor vehicle.

I later learned that in earlier times she had driven an ancient Morris Minor and was a renowned bad driver that everyone should steer clear of and allow her to rule the road.

Over a longer period, I struck up an odd friendship with the old lady and me along with Heather and the children were frequent visitors, although, they (Heather included) were given books to quietly read while she and I talked business.

Afternoon tea was something since Granny drank neither tea nor coffee. A full pot of tea was made, and woe betide anyone who attempted to leave the premises before that teapot was empty.

She never helped the tea to disappear, since the only thing she drank was a glass of tap water that came from her tank, as there was no town supply in her rural area.

To accompany the copious volumes of tea, she always had a supply of old-fashioned thick pastry jam rolls, baked until hard.

I received a telephone call from her on one occasion late in the period in which I knew her. The call from her was, "Sergeant, would you please call in here when you're coming past?"

I drove to her house and found it all quiet with no sign of her.

Walking to the entrance door, I saw a note written in pencil on the back of an envelope. The note said, "Am feeling uncommonly tired so I've gone to bed".

Going inside I knocked on her bedroom door. She said, "Is that you, Sergeant?" I said, "Yes, it's me," and pushed the door open. She was indeed in her bed, looking very tired and unwell. "Are you OK Gran, should I get a Doctor or Ambulance?"

She said, "No Sergeant, I'm starting to feel better now I've had a sleep." I left her as she was making moves to step out of her bed and waited for her to arrive in the kitchen.

She insisted that she was now well again, and I then had to suffer another pot of tea before I was set free. I think that on that occasion she expected that she was going to pass away and if so, she wished that I should find her.

Granny survived, 'in the 19th century' until her late nineties, and one day suffered a fall outside of the house. It was midwinter, and where she lived the winters often produced sub-zero temperatures.

She was found the next morning by her neighbour of about three-quarters of a kilometre distant who, looking across a large dip in the country, saw that she hadn't gathered her previous afternoon's washing; - something she never did. He investigated and found her lying on the ground, alive but freezing cold. The local ambulance driver attended, and suspecting a broken hip, attempted to place his hand up her skirt to investigate, but as cold and incoherent as she was, there was no way she was going to allow such an indignity to occur.

Granny was eventually taken to Cairns Base Hospital where I visited a couple of times. On the first visit, she wanted to talk to me alone and advised me that she wanted me to conduct her funeral service. This would be the first funeral service I had ever conducted, but I was reluctant to refuse, given our friendship and our shared faith, so I agreed.

The funeral was held in Ravenshoe, borrowing the Methodist Church for the purpose. I have attended enough funerals to have a sufficient grasp of the order of proceedings - 'Salvation Army-wise'. I borrowed the 'Army book of Ceremonies and the Salvation Army flag from the Officer at Atherton. We had the organist from our 'borrowed church', and we set out to launch into Ravenshoe's first 'Salvo' funeral. All went well, and we said our goodbyes along with a quite decent crowd from the township and surrounds as well.

The only likely hitch had occurred a few days before the funeral. Ronnie Dawson, Granny's son, who himself was an older gentleman, drove to Ravenshoe from Mareeba to see me in my office. He was very sombre and something told me he was carrying a deep dark secret. He said, "Sergeant, can I tell you something?" I said, "Sure, Ronnie, what have you to tell me?"

"Well, when we buried Dad in 1938, they put the headstone of the twin graves on the wrong side, and when they dig Mum's grave, they're gonna find Dad down at the bottom," I assured him that this would not cause a problem because these things happen from time to time, and that grave diggers have their ways and means of getting around the problem.

"It will not be an issue, but I will contact them and let them know", I said, and I did, to be faithful to Ronnie's wishes. Ronnie visibly relaxed. He had unburdened himself of this deep, dark secret that he had been carrying for around fifty years, not game to tell anyone, but worrying about just how it would all end.

Mrs Winifred (Granny) Dawson.
Cairns Historical Society.

51

A Heavy Decision.

Having in mind that I am getting on in years and it could be that in the not-so-distant future someone may be obliged, through the poor quality of my driving, to make certain decisions over my further possession of a driving license.

While in this frame of mind, I am reminded of certain dealings I had with an old chap at Ravenshoe back in the early eighties that at the time caused me to look at myself and my method of operation in dealing with the elderly and their driver's licenses.

He was a local identity, well known to Ravenshoe locals for his constant habit of driving his old utility around the district (including on the Kennedy Highway) in second gear at about 40 kilometres per hour. Needing a smoke, he'd stop wherever he was on the road and make a roll-your-own cigarette, light it, and then continue his way.

He'd done this for years and the locals gave him a wide birth.

I had heard that he'd caused more than his fair share of near misses through his driving habits, one of which involved a Council gravel truck that suddenly came across him stopped in the middle of the highway rolling a 'durry'.

There was no road accident but suffice to say the Council driver had cause to change his trousers when he returned to the depot.

In due course, there came the time for his driving license renewal, and I took the opportunity of taking him out for a driving test. I had already spoken to him on numerous occasions about his driving habits, to which he always replied, "I'm only trying to drive carefully" and no amount of talking could amend his driving practices.

During the driving test, my urging or cajoling could not get him out of second gear, nor make the ute go any faster.

I did take his license away, thus necessitating the old guy to call his son to come and take him and his ute home.

Two days later the son called to advise that his father had in fact died overnight.

He said that he (the son) held neither blame nor malice towards me because he and his family had always half expected that the old chap was going to die from a road accident through his bad driving habits and that this way, he had met his demise without affecting someone else.

Nevertheless, at some weak moments, I've wondered whether or not I should be carrying some feeling of guilt over the outcome of my decision.

Public Domain

52

An Easier Decision.

I once took an elderly lady for a driving test at the request of her daughter who told me that her Mum had just arrived in town from another far north Queensland town but where she and her driving practices were well known by the locals.

The daughter was frightened for her mother's safety and that of other road users who did not know to give her a wide berth.

We left the Atherton Police Station with the intention of driving down the main street.

She was angle parked and needed to reverse out onto the roadway, and then drive forward on the road.

I noted that she put the manual vehicle into reverse gear and then started the engine with the clutch engaged.

When on the roadway, she stopped the engine, put the car into low forward, and again started the car in the same fashion as previously.

She then remained in low gear for the journey, which, I can say was a very short test indeed. Some of those decisions to deny a renewal of a license are very easy to make.

53

A Bird In The Hand...

In country areas, the Police are expected to be ready for action or urgent service all week, night, or day. I have found that generally, the more interesting or off-key happenings are either during the night or the weekend.

One Saturday afternoon, Heather and I and the kids were relaxing at Ravenshoe when there was a knock on the front door.

It was a local resident, and he was holding a bag by the neck. This young man was a bushwalker and avid conservationist, and I said to him,

"What have you got there?"

He said, "Well in the bag I have a wedgetail eagle with a broken wing. It looks to me like someone is out in the bush shooting at birds". I made a note of where he had found it and took the bag from his hands.

Now at that time properly organized wildlife carers were a rarity, certainly in Ravenshoe, and from what I knew, there were probably none in Atherton.

Being a Saturday there would have been no Veterinary clinics open, and therefore, I was left with the injured bird until Monday morning.

My rescuer friend had bound the talons of the eagle with a strong rubber band and looking into the bag I was met by an angry, baleful-looking eye glaring back.

The presence of the eagle posed a problem. It could not spend the weekend in the bag therefore I needed a secure and suitable place where it could roost. I began telephoning around the town to find someone who could assist. I found one person who was going to Cairns the following Monday and was prepared to take the eagle to the Wildlife Service there.

I also found another local who had a large, empty walk-in bird aviary that he was prepared to make available for lodgings for our eagle. I agreed to both offers.

The owner of the aviary told me that he and his family were about to go out and that I would find nobody home when I arrived. Taking the bagged eagle, I drove to the home and entered the aviary, closing the door behind me.

I carefully emptied the bag on the floor, looking at the eyes and the wicked beak and thinking to myself, 'I'm going to have to control that head while I undo the feet from the rubber band'. So, I carefully placed my right-booted foot on the side of the head.

Squatting down, I carefully removed the rubber band, overlooking the lethality of the talons. As soon as one was freed, it moved lightning fast and latched onto the side of my bare knee. The other set sunk into the web of my right thumb and index finger.

There I was, helpless, not game to free the beak from my right boot, but in agony as all four talon claws held my other knee in a death grip while the other one immobilised my right hand. No amount of my strength could overcome the tremendous power of the talons.

I was like that for several minutes, wondering how I could remove myself from the danger when I heard the click of the front gate of the house. I saw a young girl in a Girl Guides uniform approaching the front steps. I called out to the girl while half hidden by a bush that was growing in the aviary, and she, half frightened by the sound of a male voice whose owner she could barely see, stood transfixed.

Telling her who I was, and explaining my predicament, I asked her to try to find an adult person who could come and assist me. It so happened that she lived next door, and her father appeared soon after. He hid his mirth quite effectively and joined me in the cage but our combined efforts were still insufficient to open the deadly claws.

Finally, I suggested that he find a piece of strong wire to make a loop and thread it into and behind the talons and pull them open that way. He did that, and we succeeded in opening the talons to set me free.

It was easy then to exit ourselves from the aviary, leaving the eagle inside to glare at us.

Now, to me the episode was quite serious, especially since I was injured and had goodness knows what coursing through my veins, having been injected by the eagle's talons.

The only sympathy I could draw from the town was a half-hearted 'tut-tut' from the Clinic Nurse as she injected me with an antibiotic needle.

Now ordinarily, if this were a work of fiction, this would be a good time to conclude the story, but no, there's more.

The next morning, (Sunday) the same guy was standing at our front door with another bag. This time the bag contained a white coloured owl with a broken wing.

Now owls are one of my favourite birds, and this one seemed quite placid, so I picked it up, admiring its plumage and the fact that it was so tame.

I held out my index finger to give it the chance to perch and immediately eight needle-sharp claws latched onto my finger.

The lack of sympathy of each member of my family was indeed heart-breaking as all present laughed and said, "You'd think you'd have learned something by now" and I was left to suffer alone.

We had an empty budgerigar cage, and this became the owl's lodging for the evening.

To rub salt into my extensive wounds, both birds died before the weekend passed, proving my efforts and pain to all be in vain.

54

The Attack Of The Jungle Beasts.

Speak to any person who has spent any length of time in the Tablelands rainforest, you soon find out they all know about white tail rats.

They will tell you how savage the rodents can be. Anyone who is ever bitten by one stays bitten because of the sharpness of their teeth and the strength of their jaws.

The story is told of three brothers (who won't be named), who were working in their logging camp near Ravenshoe.

Came knock-off time, and the three of them got stuck into a solid dose of alcohol to go with their corned beef sandwiches.

They were sitting on their swags as they dined, and eventually, the youngest of the three dropped off to sleep halfway through eating a sandwich.

He just lay over sideways with half the sandwich still hanging out of his mouth.

His older brothers continued to soldier on.

One brother looked over at the young fella and said to the third brother, "Look at that!"

There was the young bloke, sound asleep, sandwich hanging out of his mouth, and a couple of white tail rats eating their share of the sandwich from between his lips.

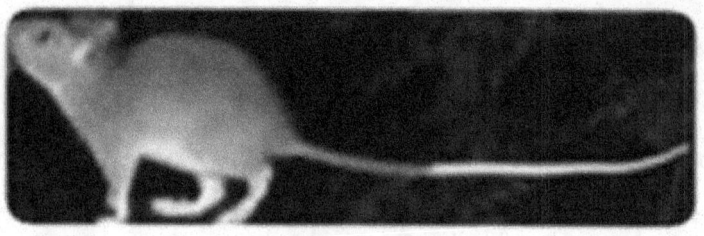

White Tailed Rat.
Photographer Unknown

55

Some Cow Bails Are More Than Meet The Eye.

As mentioned previously, the more interesting or off-key jobs seem to occur during out-of-normal working hours.

Again, at Ravenshoe one Sunday afternoon, I received a telephone call that someone had a snake inside their house and was looking for assistance to remove it.

Now I am the first to admit that snakes and I don't see eye to eye, and I share most of the population's fear of them.

I will admit to having killed more than my share of dangerous snakes over the years, no doubt because of that fear.

I thought that it being Sunday afternoon, I could take Heather and the kids out for a ride to see the snake. I also placed a bag in the boot of the car, along with a short piece of rope to tie the bag.

Ravenshoe along with many other towns has seen significant expansion since the early eighties, and much of that has been on old farms that have been sub-divided.

Our complainant's house was one of these, on an old dairy farm, but the difference with this one was that the owners had built their home out of the old milking shed, keeping one of the bails, and the bare rafters as feature points.

The worried couple took us inside and pointed up above the bails to a carpet snake that had found its way into the rafters. I figured that it should be a straightforward job to climb up on the bails, which would then make me high enough to reach the snake, uncoil it and lift it down.

Now that's all well and good, but when one makes such plans, sometimes one overlooks the innate fear of snakes, which can cause one's nerves to take a turn for the worst...

I climbed those bails and I looked that serpent square in the eye. (There would be no retreating now!).

Holding up and waving my white handkerchief with my left hand to catch the snake's eye, I quickly grabbed it behind its head with my right and unwound it from its perch. It was about that time that my nerves felt they should assist by doing what comes naturally and my knees jumped with an almighty spasm and started trembling.

My manly pride would never allow me to free my prisoner once arrested, and Queen and Country insisted that I carry out my duty at all costs. So, running the very probable grave risk of falling to my embarrassment and peril snake and all, perhaps even dying in action, I tried to convince my knees to cease shaking.

The timing was everything. Picking my moment to act between the juddering of my knees, I climbed down, breathing a huge sigh of relief once I felt terra-firma beneath my feet.

The snake went into the bag, and we managed to free it into some bushland on our way home

The things we do in the name of service to Queen, Country, and all of God's creatures.

56

A Stretch Limousine For A Police Car.

We had just finished our evening meal at Ravenshoe and were relaxing when I became aware of loud voices emanating from the main street, indicating that a brawl was in progress.

I drove down the main street to see what the town was doing. Outside of the Post Office, there was a largish crowd of indigenes gathered around two men who were just shaping up to fight.

Grabbing both the contenders, I saw that one of them was a local, and the other I did not recognise. Sending everyone else home, I quickly elicited that the stranger was from Mount Garnet. His sparring partner had said some words to him, words that escalated the situation into a fight.

The Mount Garnet lad's story agreed with the Ravenshoe boy's story, except that his presence at Ravenshoe was because he was going home and had been dropped at Ravenshoe. He had been given a lift that far and he was awaiting the arrival of someone from Mount Garnet to pick him up, but no one had arrived to do so.

I told him to climb into the police car and I would give him a lift, which he did, and I drove him to his home. He turned out to be a quiet respectful lad, who, not belonging to the Ravenshoe mob, had been picked on by the crowd to the point of having to fight.

Having dropped him off, I turned the motor vehicle back for Ravenshoe.

At a point about two-thirds of the way, travelling at 100kph a large wild pig ran out of the grass, crossing the road ahead of me. A collision was unavoidable, and it would appear that it caused the front end of the vehicle to collapse on the left-hand side. It slewed the car into a large tree standing immediately beside the road....and that is all I remember.

I awoke soon after in pitch darkness, and all I could hear was the engine coolant steam releasing and noticed that my door was refusing to open. I finally opened the door it seemed by bending it back, but the darkness did not allow me to see the damage suffered by the car.

All I could do was sit on an undented mudguard and await a passing vehicle. When a car finally arrived, I waved to the driver to stop, and long story short, the police vehicle from Mount Garnet finally arrived. The Police Officer inside the vehicle was Senr. Constable Don normally from Mareeba but relieving at Mount Garnet in the absence of the permanent O/c.

It was only then, with the assistance of his torch, that I saw the damage sustained by the car. The tree had entered the car's left side mudguard and crashed its way right through to the rear seat. I was able to show Don the dead pig, thus satisfying his query as to the cause of the incident.

Under the circumstances, especially since it was a Police vehicle involved, I suggested to him that he should take a sample of my breath for alcohol.

He immediately became embarrassed that he, a Senior Constable should be taking a sample of breath of a Sergeant, whom he knew to be a teetotaller. However, he decided that this was the correct procedure, and went ahead with the test which proved to be negative.

A tow truck was called, and the usual procedures followed their course. The wrecked car was taken to Mareeba, and it was not until a day later that I finally had the opportunity to have a proper look at the wreck.

When the time came, I could not believe my eyes. The tree entering the left side of the car had crashed right through to the differential and stretched the body to half of its length again. I was then able to reflect on how lucky my workmate was that he was not riding as a passenger in the vehicle, since he surely would have been killed by the collision.

I was uninjured except for some left-side torn rib cartilage that healed in due course. All this through a silly argument escalating into a fight in the main street of Ravenshoe.

'Stretched' Ravenshoe Police Car, 1983
Mareeba Police Photographic Section.

57

It's All A Matter Of Perspective.

My sister who lives in the southeast corner of the State dropped in to see us at Ravenshoe one afternoon.

We were glad to see her and welcomed her into our home.

At that time there was a prisoner in the watchhouse who had been locked up for drunkenness making a terrible din.

Heather and I were of course quite used to the sound and ignored it, but my sister was quite adamant that I should be getting up to check on him every time he yelled.

To add to the melee there came a telephone call from Mount Garnet.

It was the wife of that Station's Officer in Charge, to say that he and his Constable were absent but that an old chap had been reported to have passed away at his home. Could I attend?

I was just finishing my cup of tea, and Heather and I were discussing whether she and my sister might wish to visit the O/c's wife at Mount Garnet while I attended to my task there.

The next thing, my sister literally exploded, saying "I just don't understand you pair! You have a man calling out for attention in jail, and another poor man dead, and you both calmly sit here with your cups of tea and discuss it as if nothing has happened!!!

I guess she just needs to spend a little more time at a Police Station.

58

Kids In The Cop Shop.

Police kids who reside at country Police Stations get to see more than their share of 'unusual sights' from time to time, simply from the point of view of their being present at the right place at the right time.

As mentioned earlier on another page, we were initially concerned about how the things they witnessed may affect their young minds, in the case of Sharee and Brendon the opposite has occurred.

We kind of secretly congratulated ourselves as to how well our kids spoke, given their current environment, and we duly corrected them should they in any way become 'loose' with their grammar. Brendon was around the age of three and, along with other mothers and kids, Heather was sitting outside the Laura Pub awaiting her turn to be called inside to see the Flying Doctor.

All the mothers, regardless of colour, were all talking among themselves while the little kids played around the outskirts of the small crowd, – also a mixed-race group. Suddenly to Heather's consternation, floating across the air was a little white boy's voice; "Aye you fulla come ober 'ere."

She only just succeeded in hiding her surprise and realized that both of our kids in all probability had a dual vocabulary to be used according to the environment and circumstance they were in.

Our kids grew to an age of full awareness when we were at Burketown and it was interesting at times to see the effect that different incidents had on their attitudes and actions. Heather had a job at the Burketown School and loved interacting with the children and the teachers.

She was returning to the school grounds after being absent for lunch. As she attempted to walk around the corner of a building, the School Principal stopped her and said, "You may not want to walk around that corner just now".

Heather, not picking up the vibe, said "Well, that's where I was going to watch the lunchtime cricket game." The Principal replied," You may not like what you see."

Heather, walking around the corner, immediately saw Sharee involved in a fistfight with the largest boy at the school. As she watched, Sharee hit him with a round arm smash, knocking him to the ground, thus ending the fight.

Heather said, "Why haven't you stopped them?"

The Principal replied, "That boy is getting his just desserts. Ever since Sharee has been at this school, he has tormented her, tripping her up, pushing her, and generally bullying the life out of her. Today's the day he gets his comeuppance".

Being born into a white family but living in a predominantly indigenous population meant that largely it was our kids who had the above-ground pool and the trampoline etc. in the back yard.

In turn, such possessions attracted almost every child from around town from time to time. The Police Station side of our backyard happened to face the modern designed brick, ground-level watchhouse. Separating our yard from the watchhouse is a narrow laneway. Anyone could see into the watchhouse quite easily because the whole 'front' of it (the part facing our place) was made up entirely of bars and see-through steel screens. This of course meant that anyone held confined in the watchhouse was in full view of anyone peering in.

This feature became somewhat just as big an attraction to our child visitors as did both the above-ground pool and the trampoline.

Our two kids, who were quite used to seeing confined prisoners, blithely played about the yard, while the others were often distracted and spent more than a little of their time soaking up whatever kids find interesting in observing 'people in jail'.

The Yanner family is resident in Burketown, and during our time in that town, their children were in their pre-teens. There were four or five children, one child being Jason, who would later change his name to the Murri 'handle' of 'Murrandoo'.

The three older kids (which included Jason) were frequent visitors to our backyard, finding enjoyment in whatever took their fancy at that time.

One afternoon the two older boys arrived at the back gate of the property and saw there a somewhat larger number of children than usual.

Jason said, "Come on, let's go. Too many black kids here," and they left to go elsewhere. That sentiment would of course change drastically as time went by.

Our kids saw such things as busted heads, drunken brawls, naked women fist fighting outside our front gate, injured bodies from road accidents lying in the house awaiting transportation by ambulance, newly bereaved people grieving in our lounge room, and the list goes on.

One notable vision that neither one will ever forget was when they were teenagers, Sharee was about 16, and Brendon was around 14.

We were at Atherton, the residence next door to the Police Station, and the local Security Man, Phil, on his rounds had come across a woman walking down the street naked. She was obviously suffering from some kind of mental breakdown.

Phil pulled up beside her, and, wrapping her in a garbage bag he'd had in his vehicle, managed to get her into the passenger seat. He drove her to the Police Station to find that the guys on shift were out and about, absent from the Station.

His next port of call was the police residence.

I too was absent when Heather answered the door. She and Phil hustled the woman inside onto the front verandah. Now immediately at that position on the verandah, there is a door into the main bedroom, and Heather took her into there to try to find some spare clothes.

Sharee, curious as to what was going on, went into the bedroom and quickly sized the situation up, and left. Brendon was in a rear room and Sharee happened to say to him "There's a nude woman in Mum's bedroom".

Brendon, not believing her said, "Oh yair as if that's gonna happen!"

Sharee said, "If you don't believe me, go and have a look!"

Brendon did, swinging the door open with gusto, and arriving face to face with female nudity in all its raw state.

Now teenagers of that age are rarely bereft of something to say, but on this occasion, his whole energy was taken pumping enough blood to his face to blush adequately.

Such are the goings on at Police Stations and somehow or other our kids have grown up to be well-adjusted and confident members of their respective communities.

59

The 'Atherton Police Chook Cooperative.'

The Lewis's arrived at Atherton, coming from Ravenshoe on transfer towards the end of 1986. The move meant a promotion for me, and to the embarrassing surprise of the staff at Atherton Police Station, we arrived a little earlier than expected.

We found white meat chickens everywhere around the residence, and even though someone in years past had built a chook run in the yard, it was by far and away too small to accommodate such a host of birds.

We moved in, and in due course, I began working at the Station. I already knew the staff at Atherton, having been at Ravenshoe, which borders the Atherton division on the south-western side.

I found the rostered staff that morning most apologetic, obviously with something to say, and nobody wanting to be the one to say it.

Eventually, somebody said, "Max we just want to apologise for all the chooks in your yard, but while the house has been vacant, we've all been running a 'chook cooperative', all chipping in to raise 60 meat chickens that we will share amongst us when they grow large enough. We were hoping that they would be grown to size and out of here before you arrived, but as you can see, they aren't ready yet, and we're in a jam as to where to put them all."

I said, "That's not a problem, we'll run some wire netting around part of the yard and keep them confined in there for now".... and that's what happened.

Later, I was sitting in my office and became aware of a larger number of people talking in the Police Station.
Walking into the 'day room', I found all of my staff, except for the rostered officers, in old working clothes, looking purposefully about as if they were at a working bee.

A couple of them were at the photocopier and handing out pieces of paper to everyone else, and I could see that they were copying pages from an encyclopedia.

I said, "What's going on guys?"

Somebody said, "It's killing day for the chooks, Sarge and we're about to start."

I said, "What's with the bits of photocopy paper?"

He said, "Well, none of us has ever done it and we're going to go from instructions in the encyclopaedia. A couple of blokes are outside making a start".

I glanced outside and saw one of them holding onto the tied legs of one of the chickens while another was lining it up with the axe to take its head off.

The rest of them were boning up on the cleaning process—what to take, what to leave, where to cut, and where to put it. What a circus!

I said to them, "Look, I think you're going to be here all day doing this, wait here until I get dressed, and we'll do it together".

And so that's how we spent the day, and by its end, I was able to add to my resume the fact that I had succeeded in the training of a given number of Police Officers in the gentle art of chicken plucking and cleaning.

Out of it, I earned a couple of dressed and frozen chooks for the pot.

'A multitude of Chooks'
Photographer unknown.

Atherton Station, Old and New.

The old Atherton Police Station Demolished in late 1980s to make way for construction of a new station complex soon after.

'Have watchhouse, will travel' Old Atherton watchhouse loaded to travel to Herberton Historical Village as part of the rebuilding project.

The new Atherton Police Station and staff at the time including the Mareeba District Officer, Inspector Cec. Austen (Retired) (RIP). Photo (from left) Cec. Austen, Scott Neill, Kev. Wernowski, Graham Cook, Max Lewis (O/c.) Greg Crowther, Bernie Wilce.)

60

Nothing Compares With A Doggie Diet.

We had a golden Labrador cross dog at Atherton. We'd had him since we were at Laura, but at Atherton, he was a fair age and had learned to be everybody's friend.

Being part Lab., he'd always had an inbred weight problem, but now, he seemed to be pouring on the condition, even though as far as we knew, his diet had not changed.

It became so bad that we resorted to watching his actions throughout the day to find the reason for the sudden explosion. We were surprised to learn just what he was up to.

He had his own meal run most days, but Saturday was his big blowout, (having in mind that we were in the Police Residence next to the Police Station in Main Street, Atherton).

- The first visit was next door, to the Ambulance. Walk straight across the Ambulance Superintendent's highly polished floor that no one **But No One!** was permitted to besmirch.
- Over to the Forestry Office for snacks.
- At the Police Station, struggle up the steep rear steps of the old building where the police kept a supply of boiled baby potatoes for their night shift snacks.
- Over the road to the TAB where the pie cart stood and be fed a pie by a very obliging pie man, as well as occasionally a second pie from a happy TAB customer with winnings in his pocket.
- Then home for lunch... Now that's quite a day for a friendly, obese old mutt!

MAX LEWIS

Ben Lewis - Food connoisseur
Photo: Heather Lewis.

61

My Secret Son.

I've always tried to be available to those who need help or advice, whether the seeker is a member of the public or a member of my staff.

I'm proud to say that my time was on offer to everyone, night and day, and of course, due to the nature of their police work for 24 hours of the day, my staff were able to avail themselves of my time whatever the hour.

One Saturday afternoon Heather and I were doing something or other in the backyard of the Atherton residence and a member of my staff arrived from the Police Station, obviously hesitant, not sure of how he would approach me with whatever was on his mind.

He finally said, "Max, could I see you for a moment please?"

I knew then that it must have been a heavy, confidential problem, since all of my staff knew Heather very well, and could comfortably discuss operational matters in front of her.

This time, however, she was not to be allowed to hear what he had to say. I said, "What's the problem?" In a low, secretive voice.

He said, "I don't know how to say this, or whether I could tell you in front of Heather, but we've come across some young fellow out at the Tolga Pub who says he is your son".

I laughed and said, "Why would he say something like that?" He said, "Well he sounds quite convincing, and we didn't know whether to believe him or not". I said, "Well you don't need to worry about that." and I proceeded to tell Heather about our long-lost 'son'.

Then I said, "Well let's go and see my new son". We drove to the Tolga Pub, and my guys brought a young fellow out from the bar. I'd never seen him before. I said to him, "You've been mouthing off at the pub saying that you are my son. Why are you saying that?"

He said, "I'm sorry Sarge; I was just big-noting myself."

I replied, 'Well you'd better tell these Police Officers who you really are, and stop big-noting yourself, because, under no circumstances do I wish for you to be a member of my family."

It's amazing what some people will do once they have a belly full of alcohol to build themselves up in the eyes of their friends.

Geeze mate, just 'cos y're a pom and you wear a stupid bloody hat doesn't make ya speshul. If you're Boy George, then the geezer in charge down at the Cop shop is my old bloody man! Sheez! Next you'll tell me you're Prince Bloody Charles!

62

Life Turns A Corner After Atherton.

We thoroughly enjoyed our sojourn in Atherton. Many tales came out of the seven years we lived and served there.

I was promoted to Senior Sergeant, to coincide with the Station commencing a 24-hour Policing service.

Both of our kids completed their High School studies, Sharee left home to further her education and ultimately found herself joining the Police Service.

Brendon commenced studies at Innisfail in a new course aimed at preparing young people for recruitment in the Queensland Police Service.

He was later to be offered a position with Telstra in Townsville and began climbing the ranks within that Corporation.

Brendon would, some years later grow tired of the frustrations of working for Telstra.

He saw an opportunity, and ten years ago became a FIFO worker at Groote Eylandt and is currently working at the level of Shift Foreman.

I was again promoted, this time to Inspector, and transferred to the Townsville Regional Office as a Regional Projects Officer. So ended my life as a country Police Officer.

Heather and I retired in 1999.

You hear many, not all, former Police Officers say, "If I had the chance, I'd do it all again".

I'm one of those, mindful of the fact that *'The Job'* as we call it, is a very different one to that which we joined years ago, and in which we were proud to serve.

Who can say whether it's as good as, or better than the Service that we retirees whimsically call 'the good old days?'

Our daughter Sharee is one of the modern Police, although she has now arrived at Commissioned Officer level, having also done her time in several country locations.

My advice to any young Police Officer seeking advice about which way to head to have a satisfying career would be as follows...

It matters not one bit whether you are Catholic, Protestant, or indeed any religion, neither as a member of a Masonic Lodge (or any other) to succeed in the Queensland Police Service.

There are many exciting jobs within the Police Service, but if your wish is for variety, independence, great stories and yarns, and the making of genuine forever friendships to tell your Grandkids about, get yourself a bush station!

Heather and I offer both greetings and a sincere thank you to the multitude of people whom we have had the honour to meet, serve, become friends with, and together shared coffee and yarns. We have been truly blessed because you have all enriched our lives, and those of course, of our now adult children

The Forgotten O/c. (Officer In Charge).

A Policeman is often mentioned for his exploits out on the street,
The difficult and nasty jobs that happen on the beat.
For the loyalty to duty when bad incidents are rife
And the community is suffering from criminals and strife.

And he collects a swag of comments how he bravely took the stand
For what he thought was honest against pressures on every hand.
How for 'The Job' he suffered the effect of stress and strain
And fought tears of frustration and grief for someone's pain.

Well, those things are so often true in an officer's career.
There's much that goes unmentioned, some things you'll never hear.
But the part most often overlooked, the most central in his life,
Is that endured in partnership, the part played by his wife.

She suffers his frustrations and feels like no other can
The way the world wears harshly the charity of her man.
She bears his rough impatience when the day has been unkind,
And supports his stand of courage when the world wants to be blind.

She's content to take the second seat and allow her man to pride
When the thing done was on equal shares and she was by his side.
Sometimes she bears the brunt of jibe when unkind things are said,

When out of loyalty she speaks for right but could silent be instead.

Well, never let it now be said how often men forget.
And neglect our wives' enjoyment of the praise they should rightly get.
You've worked beside us through the years to help realize our plan
Your reward no more simply than to be there with your man.

We may not be forthcoming with our praise for a job well done,
And we may often be impatient when our day has badly run.
But we'd like to tell you 'thank you' you've really stood the test,
Well, for being such a great O/c. put simply, you're the best!

Max Lewis

VALE CECIL ROY AUSTEN (RIP).

Regional Superintendent (Retired) Cec. Austen (RIP)
Photo: Mareeba District Photographic Section

From time to time in life, one comes across a person who ultimately becomes a model and inspiration to those he or she has influenced in day-to-day working and living.

When I was at the concluding stages of this book, we lost such a person who to me was both the above and more, and my experience was shared among many of my police colleagues for the simple reason that this person was our 'boss'.

VALE CECIL ROY AUSTEN (RIP).

Cecil Roy Austen was a Police Commissioned Officer who was looked up to and admired, I am sure, by all who encountered him.

He helped shape my career in its latter stages as a leader and manager, my day-to-day work, and my conduct in dealing with other members of humankind.

I was fortunate to have had Cec as my boss three times during my career in the Queensland Police Service: Once as my District Officer at Mareeba as I served as Officer in Charge of two consecutive police Stations on the Atherton Tableland.

The second was when I was temporarily seconded to a management unit in Cairns as the Police Service underwent major changes. and then soon after when Cec was the Regional Superintendent of the Far Northern Region before his retirement.

I believe I am in a sufficiently knowledgeable position to state that Cec and his wife Hillary had/have as their inspiration a deeply spiritual faith that guided and empowered their lives and influenced their positive dealings with people, all of whom were treated as equals regardless of rank or social standing.

The Retired Police Association has lost a valuable member and great friend in Cec's passing, but those who were close to him are secure in the knowledge and belief that he is now in a better place enjoying his eternal reward for a life of valuable service.

About the Author

Author: Inspector (Retired) Max Lewis
Photo: Jill Hardy

Although he was born in the country (Nanango Queensland) Max Lewis was raised from childhood in the City of Brisbane. Leaving school at the tender age of 14 years, Max struggled in several jobs due to his immaturity until reaching the age of around 20 when he finally could hold down a job. In 1966 he joined the Queensland Police Service.

Serving some 33 years he rose to the rank of Inspector but chose to serve in predominately country police stations where he and his wife and family also participated in the day-to-day functioning of whatever country town they found themselves.

Although Max grew up in the city he shows in his book how, through community participation, the enjoyment of hearing bush yarns and stories, and the interaction with truly country people can convert a 'city boy' into 'A Country Cop' at heart.

www.ingramcontent.com/pod-product-compliance
Lightning Source LLC
Chambersburg PA
CBHW070250010526
44107CB00056B/2414